```
BIO        Spence, John C.
E
605        A diary of the Civil
.S74         War
1993
BIO Spe
```

BELMONT UNIVERSITY LIBRARY

Watkins College
of Art & Design

A DIARY OF THE CIVIL WAR

by John C. Spence

Published by
The Rutherford County Historical Society
Murfreesboro, Tennessee
1993

Copyright 1993
by
The Rutherford County Historical Society

Printed by Williams Printing Company
Nashville, Tennessee

Library of Congress Catalog Card Number 93-084827

John Cedric Spence
(picture provided by Eric S. Chamberlain)
Natchez, Mississippi

Elizabeth Spence
(picture provided by Eric S. Chamberlain)
Natchez, Mississippi

About The Author

John Cedric Spence was born November 14, 1809 in Murfreesboro, Tennessee. His father, John Spence, was born in Ireland, and his mother, who was Mary Chism, was born in Virginia. John Spence, along with his brother, Marmon, came to Middle Tennessee the same year that John Cedric was born.

John Cedric's school days extended over a period of about seven years. Eighteen months of this time was spent at Hopewell Academy. Within this period he obtained a fair knowledge of the English language and learned the rudiments of natural sciences. John relates in his **Annals of Rutherford** that he served an eight-year apprenticeship in the store of his Uncle Marmon. He tells an interesting story of how in September of 1831 at the age of 22 he along with his friend D.D. Wendell, began an extensive journey through the sparsely-settled West Tennessee.

In 1832 John Cedric went to Sommerville, Tennessee where he opened a store of his own. He remained in business there until 1847 when he moved to Memphis, Tennessee. He continued in business in Memphis until 1849 at which time he returned to Murfreesboro. Here he remained in the mercantile business until his health failed.

John Cedric Spence started the Red Cedar Bucket Factory in Murfreesboro in 1854. The factory at that time was located at the present site of the City Police Department. Later, the factory moved to a location south of the old freight depot.

There was a carriage manufacturing establishment in the Jacob-Hancock two-story residence on the north side of College Street just east of the present Cavalry Bank. Mr. Spence bought that house and had it moved on wooden wheels to the present site of the Discovery House on North Maple Street. This became his home.

John was married to Elizabeth Spence, their family names being the same, on September 16, 1834 in Murfreesboro. John became a member of the Methodist Episcopal Church on October 15, 1882. At that time J.B. Plummer was the pastor. John was always a Whig as long as that party existed. At the outbreak of the Civil War, he bitterly opposed secession; however, as the war escalated his influence and feelings were with the South.

Marmon Spence, John Cedric's uncle, was one of Murfreesboro's most noted citizens. He served as mayor from 1834 to 1835 and became the owner of a large number of buildings in the area of the Public Square. Some of his heirs who live in New York still own and administer 19 of these buildings.

John Cedric was an avid and very capable chronicler, not knowing whether any of his annals would ever be read or published. He was possessed with a deep sense of history and felt a constraint to spend hundreds of hours in writing his manuscripts.

The Rutherford County Historical Society would like to think that it is fulfilling John Cedric's dream as it publishes his annals.

Foreword

The Rutherford County Historical Society came into possession of John Cedric Spence's **Diary of the Civil War** through the courtesy of Eric S. Chamberlain of Natchez, Mississippi. Mr. Chamberlain, a descendant of John C. Spence, discovered this diary in an attic of one of his elderly relatives following her death. Realizing the value the diary would have for interested citizens of Rutherford County, Mr. Chamberlain was willing to part with it. The journal that contained this diary was in manuscript form and fully legible even though it was over 100 years old.

The reader will notice errors in spelling and sentence structure. However, the Society felt it was important to retain the style in which Spence had written. The reader will appreciate the fidelity given by the Society in preserving Spence's style and methods of expressing his ideas.

Apology

Having for many years past been in the habit of noting down little events for future refference, things that may be of service to me and frequently things that would be of but little to myself or any one else. Such is habit. I commenced this Diary at the beginning of the trouble in the country with the thought that something **would** occur that I should like to recollect for future refferences.

Not intending to make my notes so extended as they have turned out. When I got in, found the field so large, could not resist the numerous notices of occurences that has taken place during this unfortunate War.

It may be a source of satisfaction at some future day to look over the grounds we have travled — and compare the past with the present.

Not having any employment in the army or out of it, consequently had **time** to spare. In fact so much of it that it was rather a drug. In this way, thought proper to use some of the capital in which I was so rich. Spending an hour or so noting down little occurrences that should happen.

These notes are not intended for the public eye, but possibly some one may have curiossity to take a glance at them. If so they can read and let them go for what they are worth.

The principle events that is herein, notice, has taken place in and around Murfreesboro.

I do not intend to confine myself entirely to this locality. There are other points which is familiar to all. Something can be collected of interest.

I have endeavored to arrive at the truth as near as circumstances would admit. At any rate enough so to answer the purpose these notes were intended.

To note every thing that has taken place for the past four years about Murfreesboro would fill a large volume. One that would make a yank blush if he had any shame in his face.

I have explained my position sufficiently to be understood at least by myself.

Author

Diary

In the year, 1860, it became necessary to nominate candidates for the Presidency. John Bell, of Tennessee, was the first to be nominated and the true union candidate. "The union, constitution, and the enforcement of the laws." The next was the Democratic which met at Charleston, S.C. Here they did not agree; adjourned to Baltimore to make nominating at this place. They again disagreed and made a split in the party. Douglass was nominated by the Northern Section, and the Brackenridge party adjourned to Richmond. Here they completed the nomination. These two candidates were seen as true Democratis. Each was contended to be the better, and each contended that the opposite was for breaking up the union.

Immediately after, a convention was held at Chicago which nominated A. Lincoln, the Republican or Abolition candidate, a man of not much notariety, scarcely ever having been heard of out of his immediate section. But one that could be worked with ease, a kind of **putty man.** He went by the cognomen of "Honest Old Abe, the rail splitter," just the kind of man the Republican party most needed for the present emergency.

It will now be seen that we have four candidates in the field, all ready booted and spurred for the great Presidential race. Each with his necessary document, or passport, and, of course, all have the true construction of the constitution. The word is given and off they start.

Among the hustlers in the race we find one Andy Johnson, head groom in the Brackenridge Stable, rubbing down for the Southern state rights nag. The way he was run in the south and when taken North, he was run as the true Democrat and only Union man.

Douglass was run as a National man, both North and South, and also, was Bell. These two men were both sound on the constitution, but not good in a race.

The race came off on the 4th of Nov. following. The judges gave in favor of A. Lincoln, he being the foremost man. Brackenridge the next, then, Douglass Bell he was distanced.

It is clearly seen that the Democratic party was the cause of the great split in the union. For had the party remained together and not divided, in all probability the Republican party would have been defeated. And then, there would not have been any secession.

Well! The election is over. The die is cast. We must now look to the result in future.

It will be remembered the North and South have for years past been at War in words on the subject of Warring. This year, 1860, we had four candidates in the field. One of them formidable, being the leader of the Republican or Abolitians party. This party the South fought hard against and declared if elected would be a sufficient cause for them to withdraw from the Union. Thus, matters wore on, each battleing for its own candidate. The day came, the elections over, and the result proved to be A. Lincoln, the abolition candidate elected.

The South, true to its promise, now determined they would withdraw from the union and, forthwith, went to work to accomplish that object. By way of remark would say here the south was acting a little hasty in the matter for on examination it was found on a joint ballot in congress there was a majority of six against the incoming party. So if the matter had have remained, Pnt. Lincoln would have proved harmless for any measure he may have proposed. Could be voted down having a majority against him.

In this War South Carolina took the first step in the matter. Other states followed immediately after. Order of secession of the States— South Carolina Decem. 20/60, Missi. Jany 9/61, Alabama Jany 11/61, Florida Jany 11/61, Georgia Jay 19/61, Louisiana Jay 26/61, Texas July 1/61, Vir. April 17/61, Arkans - May 6/61, North Carolina May 20/61, Tennessee June 8/61 (11 in all).

Buchanan, who was president at the time appeared to favor the scheme or at least he did not seem to interfere with the movement of the southern states in their plans for secession from the union. He may have looked at the matter as rather a threat that would not be attempted to be carried out.

Matters continued on hastily in this way. The seceeded having voted themselves out of the union, a convention was called and **Jefferson Davis,** was nominated and elected provisional president. Being notified to that effect, he hastened to take his seat and administer the government.

A constitution was formed, which was nearly the same as the U.S. with a fiew exceptions. Matters being thus asauged to carry on business in an active manner, the first thing done after Davis assumes authority was to secure the Forts and all public property that lay in their teritory.

Business of this kind moved on at a rapid rate between the time of the election of Lincoln and the time of his inauguration as president.

The Southern States had now formed themselves in a confedaracy, called the **Confederate States of America.**

The Confederate capital, being established at Montgomery, Alabama. Members to congress was elected and matters assumed a business appearance. Commenced enacting laws and regulations for their better government and establishing the army regulations and munitions of war.

The time was now drawing nigh for Prst. Lincoln to take hold of the reins of government. He is now making his way to Washington. As he goes makes small speeches, adapted to the section of country he passes. Something to tickle the fancy. He was feeling his way and like the boy who had to travel through a grave yard he felt scared and had to whistle loud to keep from seeing a ghost. As he neared the capital he became more frightened at something, but, as luck would have it, he reached the place, it is said, in disguise, having assumed the Scotch costume of highlander. Be this as it may from his little speeches it indicated he was disposed to blow hot and cold with the same breath. Or at least, he wishes to shew favor to both sections of the United States. He saw things was getting in a knotted condition. However, under all these circumstances, he was duly inaugurated Prst of the United States.

Things moved on during the winter without much of interest with the exception of each party commenced the preparation of War implements.

Offers was made by the South for an adjustment of the matter. Commissioners were sent to Washington for that purpose, but little attention was paid to them. They returned and reported progress.

Nothing now remains but to commence hostility.

The southern people put themselves in an attitude of defence. They commence the preparation of Forts and Batteries in and about Charleston, S.C., still, with the hope something might turn up to stop hostilities. They were not long in getting fortified at Charleston and ready for an attact. And thus, they remain in the situation for some time.

The winter of 1861 wore off. Prst Buchanan was still occupying chair of chief magistrate. He did not seem disposed to pay much attention to what was going on, but formed the idea of getting a bad job off his hands and turning it over to one better qualified to fill the the office.

Peace measures was introduced into congress, by Crittendon of Ky., but the compromises was not of such a nature as to allay the feelings of the people of the South. This was toward the close of session of Congress.

A. Lincoln now takes the reins of government in hand, puts out his proclamation, which was got off in such style that it was hard to understand what course he was disposed to take. The South still in a war attitude. March 4, 1861.

Of the seceeded states, up to this date, six had retired from the union; five still remaining verry much agitated, and among that number we find Tennessee. A call session of the Legislature was made by Gov Harris to take into consideration the great question of the country, and a day was set apart to hold an election. The question was "For Convention or no Conventions." Also, to elect members to conventions. Candidates were elected, in case there would be a convention. No convention carried, by over *sixty two thousand*. So, at this time, Tennessee stood square up for the union. This takes place some time in the month of February, 1861.

Subsequently, the Legislature was called again by Gov. Harris. It passes the ordinance of secession. The ticket on this occassion was

Separation and Representation. This takes place in the month of June following. Tennessee has made a complete somersault—by some seducive means being used. It now votes for secession. Over **Fifty nine Thousand**. It was the last on the list to leave the Union

Democracy had been in the ascendency for several years in this state, and at the time of the secession vote it was large in the majority—comment would be unnecessary.

We go back to July election in Tennessee or even a little further-at a time, when, the word secession was odious to all good citizens and to those that were not so good. At this time we had among us a young man from South Carolina who was teaching a Military School. He had been at home in his vacation. Takes hold of the new doctrine—Secession. Returns and endeavors to scatter the principle among the people. Introduces a company of military boys with guns. Every day have private meetings. They wore badges on their hats, (blue cockade). By this means a fiew seeds of secession was scattered and took root. Must it be said! To the best recollection of all that wore cockades not a single man belonged to any other party than that of Democracy. This is brought in to shew at what time and how secession was introduced among us—and what class was most susceptable of its effects.

At this time, all the Southern members had withdrawn from the congress of the United States, with a fiew exceptions and among the fiew, A. Johnson is found remaining. He, by some means peculiar to the man, takes this back tract, makes a flaming, union speech in congress at the time, had some traits of a redeeming character, but after all, it was Andy!! His nation developing.

April 1, 1861

By April 1, 1861, things had put on a strong appearance of war. Preparations was going on in a lively manner.

South Carolina, having made itself ready for some demonstration, becomes impatient. Makes a formal demand of the forts at Charleston to surrender. Coln Anderson, the commandant at the time and occupying, refuses to do so; thus, it remained until the morning of 12th April. The ball opened at Charleston by firing on Fort Sumter. The first cannon that was fired must have had an astounding affect on the ears and nerves of the inhabitants of the place. A kind of death knell. The blow is struck for wield, or for woe.

However, the cannonading continued nearly all day on Fort Sumpter. Coln Anderson, occupying, and resisting, with all the means in his power. At last the walls was beat in and set on fire by shells. It was now surrendered to the Charlestonians, and Anderson and his men, who fought heroicly, were relieved. There were vessels lying off the Charleston harber, but they failed to render assistances.

Up to this time, Virginia had not passed the order of secession, but, in a very short time did, April 17. She now numbers among the confederate states. Both sections of the country are at this time making lively preparation for resistance.

Calls for volunteers by both sides is made and responded to in a lively manner. Prs Lincoln issues his proclamation, calling on the states for **seventy five thousand men**. This made people open their eyes to see what course to take. Lincoln called it a Rebellion. The south called it Revolution.

Here seems to be a split. A man is almost compelled to take sides in the matter. His feelings promping, he reasons thus: "I am a northern born man; my family and friends are there. I choose that course." The other, "I am a southern raised man; my family and friends are there. For that reason I am more attatched to the south." The latter man is as good a union man, in sentiment and feeling, as the former. The thing is started this way, in a tender manner, and, in the course of time each will call the other hard names and the worst epithets that can be applyed. If he is south, the word sesesh, Rebel, or the North—Yankee, Black Abolitionist. As war continues, hatred increases.

April 20, 1861

By April 20, 1861, volunteers are gathering all over the country and our town was not behind in that thing. A company was raised by Stephen White. It was independant; left for Virginia on their own account. Shortly after, another raised by Mr. Ledbetter Jr., and in a short time several others was also raised.

When the war first started it was thought by both Northern and Southern people, that it would not last over ninety days at most. So Lincoln made his call for ninety days. All parties entered as a matter of frolic, had very little idea that any fighting would be done.

Guns and amunitions was about to prove a difficult matter to procure. So men/citizens put to work. Salt peter cans was searched for and, in fact, the whole county ransacked for materials in the way of amunition.

A small gun establishment was started at Murfreesboro by a company conducted by T. Robertson and Richard Sanders. They had several hands employed and could turn eight or ten very good rifles per day. They had a large number of barrels forged out by the smiths. Also had an agent Stephen Singleton, whose business was to collect all the old rifle guns that was of any size or such as would make a Missippi Rifle. In this way great many guns was furnished. They had got in the way of making a neat finished gun. Soldiers were supplyed with this arm.

Other branches of business was also carrying on the making of catridge boxes, straps, and belts. J. Bohmes had a contract of this kind—Ambulances, a two wheel concern, put on springs, some what in the manner of a covered cart, to be used with one horse. Had a neat appearance, and, I suppose, answered the purpose intended. Havnissor of this business, W.G. Garrett, was the principle.

There were several persons engaged in making what was called an army wagon. This was a small, two horse concerns, not calculated in carrying a verry heavy load. Other minor articles that was necessary to make up camp equipage was made here. There were quite an extension armory built at Nashville for the manufacture of guns and everything else that should be needed. They had got to manufacture percussion caps quite extensive here. A large number of well finished cannon were also made at this place. A man by the name of Brinnon was principle.

So, it will be seen, that necessity is the mother of invention. If these things that is being made here and other places over the country could be procured from a distance with ease, scarcely an article would be made here and the argument would be we have no machinery scarcely any material and no artisans to work. Where there is a will there is a way. If the Southern people had depended more on their home for their wants and less on the north, they would this day have been more independant. But we have been depending on the North for almost every thing we want - even to brooms and axe handles.

There is no country so well adapted to live within itself as the state of Tennessee. The best of water power, every species of timber, of the best, for all purposes. Iron, Copper, Lead, Marble will add gold and silver. Beside this, where is the country that is superior in agriculture? As a whole, all that is needed, is the energy to develop the wealth of the county.

May 1st, 1861

It will be seen our date is advancing. There is quite a commotion over the country. Volunteers are being raised, but all independant, individual enterprises. The all important question with Tenn. has not come up. She has been once tryed and the question will have to come again. There is a heavy influence working in the mind of the people. Still, a distant hope that something may turn up that will stop blood shed. The Lincoln call causes a hesitation. Tenn. knows she is loyal; fears nothing; wishes to be at peace with all. But, the call is on all loyal states for its share of men to allay a rebellion. Who rebells! My nearest neighbor! Must spill his blood? I stop. I hesitate.

The Subject of War is now being thought. More of the people begin to look at the matter. Volunteers are now being raised by different persons. J.B. Palmer has offered his servises and has raised a large respectable company. Also, Adison Mitchell and several others leave in a short time for the camp of instruction—which is at a place near the Kentucky line, Camp Trousdale. These were the first companies that left here for the defense of Tennessee. Two other companys previously mentioned went to Virginia to join the army there. They were all a gallant set of boys, full of life.

May 10, 1861

Tennessee, in May of 1861, is still in the union, but quite a change of affairs have come over the people since the President's Proclamation. It had been plain that Tennessee could not stand on retreat ground. It had, either to espouse the cause of the North or the South, and the general feeling was tendency to the latter. Great changes was going on in the mind of the people. They began to feel that this was likely to turn out an abolition war, if war it shall be, and in that case will resist to the last.

All parties are now taking a lively part in making preparation. Altho many engaged in the matter not altogether satisfied that they were doing right; but, thought as a matter of necessity for the general good. Those that voted union in Feb. last, as well as those that voted contrary, all gave a helping hand.

The armys in Virginia was increasing in size and importance—but, even at this time, it was thought that there would be but little fighting—that the matter would die off in a short time. This was the feeling.

The Federals or (Abolitionist), make an order to have Cairo (at the mouth of the Ohio river) well fortified, which is an important point in many respects.

May 20, 1861

Scarcely any thing worth noting. Still hear of war preparation through different parts of the country. The Southern, or Confederate army, are commencing fortifications at different posts. One place, Island No 10, on the Mississ. River. And just above that place are making a fort, called Fort Pillow. These places seem to be good positions to command the river and stop navigation at least for a time.

The Confederate army are still increasing. At Camp Trousdale, from the best information, are all in good health and spirits—are kept close at drill every day—the friends of the boys are making visits every week to them, taking them clothing and boxes of something to eat. So, war is not such a bad thing after all? They have no fears, are satisfied they can **whip** two **Yankees** to one and would not wish to engage a less number. Being in a war camp has a tendency to make men courageous and defiant and may add somewhat devilish.

Can hear of Federal forces comeing south of Louisville under the command of Gen. Buell. They are moving slowly toward Nashville now at what is called Melrose Hill and other places in that neighborhood.

Does this not break the nutrality of Ky?

June 1, 1861

It has been a matter of doubt with the southern soldiers whether either party had the right to enter the teritory of Ky., as she claimed to be on nutral ground and not taking sides. At all events, the southern army took that view and did not enter. But, seeing that the Northern army had taken that privilege, they consider the way is open to them. Hence, they move to a place called Bolinggreen Ky. and then commence fortifying the place. This town lies immediately on the Louisville & Nashville road. Up to this time the Southern army did not attempt to pass the line.

Fort Donaldson, on the Cumberland River, was also constructed by the Confederate army and is thought to be a pretty strong position. It is manned and in readiness for any invasion.

June 8, 1861

The great question with Tennessee has again come up in June of 1861. The vote will be taken whether its destiny is with the North or the South. As has been previously mentioned, the aspect of things have undergone quite a change of late.

Yes! Tennessee has gone with the South, for weal or woe. It has voted **Separation** and Representation, **over fifty nine thousand** majority—now stands among the states that has withdrawn from the union. A Confederate!

A hard fight takes place a short distance from Island No 10 (ten). The Federals are repulsed with a pretty heavy slaughter. They were drove back to their boats. This one of the first that has taken place in the west. The Confederates followed them up for several miles, called battle of Bellmont.

The fortifications at Bolinggreen was progressing in a vigorous manner almost to completion, but tis found they can be of little service for the enemy can pass them on either side and leave them miles to the right or left, if they should be disposed to come to Nashville but military men know best.

Buell is not Idle. He is preparing his way and making slow advances on the road to Nashville and Bolinggreen or some other point. May hear from him in a short time.

A great many articles are being manufactured at Nashville and other points. Such as cannon and gun carriages, harness, sabers, rifles, apparel for soldiers. The chance of getting any thing in this time being cut off. Numbers of blankets were made of carpeting or havre sacks.

All this business was going on during the summer in a lively manner. Friends and relations were busy making up clothing and sending to the soldiers by the quantity. In fact, nothing was lacking—and many a good thing in the shape of sweet meats was sent to the soldiers.

Among other things, not unfrequently, a jug of **Robertson County** was not forgotten. Frequent visits of friends to the camps. Occaisionally a furlough home for a short time.

Such was the first essays in soldiering. All well satisfied; with their condition, nor wished it better.

The whole month of June being taken up in this way nothing worthy of particular note. So the time may be advanced up to—

July 1st, 1861

By July 1, 1861, matters began to change. Could hear of frequent skirmishes in different portions of the country. Volunteering was now going on in a lively way almost every where. The armies were swelling to size and importance.

Mail service now stoped coming to the south from the northern states. There now begins to be a stir among the people. Those whose sympathy were with the North commenced turning their face in that direction, and just here there seemed to be a division. Then even some, who were not satisfied as to the course things were taking, they shut their mouth and said nothing. They disliked the idea of making a split in the union as such appeared to be the tendency.

As has been mentioned the confederates were occupying and fortifying at Bolinggreen, Ky. Also building fast, Fort Donaldson on the Cumberland River. And Fort Henry on the Ten River. These were rather put up in a temporary manner and armed with the necessary quantity of guns and men.

As yet, there was nothing to make war irksome to the soldier. Everything to all appearances was going on in a easy manner. Some of the more aspiring was electioneering among the soldiers to be promoted to higher office. The friends of the soldiers were making daly visits to the camps from a distance carrying with them, clothes and lots of letters and boxes of little nice things from mothers and sisters to eat and drink. It was almost like the orientals in their anual visits to Mecca to worship their heathern gods.

The people at home at Murfreesboro never once dreaming that they should ever hear the roar of cannon, the rattle of muskets, or the groans of the dying—to see or hear any of this they would most likely have to travel hundreds of miles to witness such tragedys.

There are thousands who are lending a helping hand in this matter and are at the same time not satisfied in their own mind of the propriety of the course pursuied, but are not disposed to be out done by their neighbor in shewing a patriotic feeling. Mankind is a strange compound at best.

July 10, 1861

We turn our attention in the direction of Virginia to Manassas. Preparation is being made by both armys to bring on an engagement. Each feel equal to the task. Genl Lee, of the Confederate, and Genl. Mc Clelland, of the Union, are the two competitors in the coming contest. They are gradually drawing nearer each other.

The Southern boys, having got themselves into the belief that each one of them were equal to three Yankees in a fight, were willing to have the meeting. With this odds against them a fight is what they want.

The Union men, as they called themselves, many of them feel equally brave and fully satisfied in their minds that they could carry the day, as they had decided the advantage in numbers of men and superior arms. To sustain the idea they thought to make a frolic or jubilee of the thing full of confidence of their ability to conquer and scatter the rebels to the four winds.

Great numbers, Gentlemen and Ladies and members of Congress and citizens generaly came out of Washington City to witness contest now about to take place. Tis said quantities of wines and confectionaris were brought along to make cheer on one side,—and for the other, wagon loads of **Hand Cuffs** for the vanquished.

Scene, Battle of Manassas

Lines of Battle being now formed both defiant—one relying upon its ability to conquor three to one—the other in the overwhelming numbers of men. Slight skirmishing commences along the lines—officers activly engaged, carrying dispatches from their Genls—manouvring and encouraging their men. Now and then a cannon is either heard to the right or left of lines. Now vollies of musketry rattle all along the lines. Cannon now belching forth their deadly messonges. The lines approach near each other. The word is given to charge! They charge and in return are recharged again, and thus, the combatants keep up the fight. At times, from hand to hand, nearly the whole day. The struggle becomeing disperate on both sides.

The Confederate soldiers fighting like deers and as determined. They once more make a deadly charge on their foe and at the same moment poured in a galling fire. At this their opponents faltered—wavered—and finally gave way. They threw down their guns, napsacks, blankets, and every thing else that would impede a a run. They took the tract in the direction of Washington in double quick and left the field all in the hands of the rebel army. In this display of racing several members of Congress came very near being distanced. In fact, one was. He had to be put in a rebel stable and be rubbed down for several months before he could be returned in good running order.

Such was the fright of the Northern soldiers that some of them ran so far that they never returned again. They became alarmed about the safety of Washington City. Reinforcements was brought to guard the capital. It was thought if the rebel soldiers had not been so much fatigued from the days fight and had continued the races that Washington could have been easily taken at this time.

We now go back to the battle ground. Here we find the rebels feasting and drinking all sorts of good liquors that had been brought there by the Union people for the intended jolifications. It seemed that the rebels were enjoying themselves at the expense of union men. But as for the **hand cuffs**, they did not appear disposed to partake. They satisfied of having gained the day and of seeing the **Bull Run** to Washington—

After this part of the affair was passed, it became necessary to look to the disposition of the wounded and dead, this having been a hard contested battle. The killed and wounded on each side was great. From this time matters quieted down for a time. The Yankee army had in this contest became demoralized and would require some time to get matters straitened up. They lost no time in further arrangements to the prosecution of the war.

This success had a tendency to give the confederate army encouragement. They moved on with more vigor in their preparation. Recruiting in all sections now increased. No difficulty to raise a regiment of soldiers.

Besides this there was verry little of interest in and around Murfreesboro. The soldiers were progressing with their fortifications at Bolinggreen in a leisure manner. Also drilling their men.

We can hear of the Yankee army making slow movements from Louisville in the direction of Nashville, and we have a feeling that they will have a lively time getting there if ever.

This army, that is advancing this way, is under the command of Genl Buell.

We will now pass over a space of time not having any thing that would be worth note. We will presume that all partys are engaged in working on their fortifications and drilling their soldiers and getting matters generally in a condition for the offensive and defensive—and that the friends at home are busy in making up clothing for winter use of the soldiers. By the time this shall have been completed the balance of the summer and fall season will have run out.

December 1st, 1861

We now advance date up to Dec. 1, 1861, having quite a space intervening. Nothing of importance, has transpired worthy of note, but still an anxiety in the minds of the people of what would next take place. The purchase of goods had stoped some time since by the merchants that were in the habit of getting supplies from the North. The stocks were reducing verry much. Our carriage shops were in the manufacture of ambulances, wagons, and harnesses for the use of the army. Some engaged in making cartridge boxes, belts and one establishment making cavalry saddles. In fact, more or less every branch of mechanical were engaged in fitting up army articles. Our little gun factory was pushing on matters in quite a lively way.

During the fall, we had some confederates soldiers stationed in the neighborhood, about three miles out at A. Millers place. Established as a camp of instruction, they proved to be a little troublesome to him, as they would now and then take a cedar rail from his fence and burn it. This hurt his feelings, but he ought not complain as he was strongly in favor of secession. However they did not remain at this place long. They were ordered to some other point to the great relief of Alfred. Soldiers have ways peculiar to themselves. All restraints are thrown off when in the army.

We secure an order for the establishment of a hospital for the Confederate army at this place. The Union university was selected for that purpose and immediately fitted up for the reception of the sick soldiers.

There was a field for the Ladies to operate, which they did with a good will. They collected large quantities of goods of every description— formed a sewing society for the benefit of the hospital. In a short time, large quantities of clothing was made: sheets for bunks, ticks and straw to put in, stoves, kettles, pans, and every thing that should be necessary for hospital purposes was procured.

Every thing was fitted up in a neat and comfortable manner by the ladies and made ready for the reception of sick soldiers.

The Ladies formed a hospital society, or (Soldiers Relief Society). Mrs. L.H. Carney was elected president of said society, and Mrs. Jas Avent, appointed treasurer. This society had been formed some months previous to this date. Large quantities of clothing were made up and sent off to the different portions of the army—Virginia and other places. Dr King was appointed the head surgeon of the hospital.

About the twentieth of the month, a large number of sick soldiers was sent forward from Nashville and other places to this hospital. This being the first introduction of hospital service at this place. All ever on the go and anxious to see who could render the most aid to the sick, having quite a store room of clothing. As fast as the soldiers would come they were washed and a suit of clean clothes were put on them. A comfortable bunk assigned them, and upon the whole, a hospital did not appear so bad after all.

The meal times were regular and of the best that was to be had. A long table was spread with a clean cloth, plates, knives, and forks, and other necessary things to set off, and a plenty to attend the wants of the soldiers. In fact, it was not far behind a second rate Hotel, and all felt a patriotic feeling for the comforts of the soldiers. If there were a chance for a man to get well, he had it here.

In this manner things passed on to the close of the year. Nothing transpiring of much note.

January 1st, 1862

It is January 1, 1862 and we now commence a new year. The troubles begin to thicken. Can hear of slight battles at different points but nothing serious to either party. Some fighting in the mountains of Virginia, also along the sea coast. The Federal forces have gathered quite strong at the junction of the Ohio and the Mississipi Rivers. From appearances, we may look for some hard fighting in a short time as the union and Confederate men shew a determination each to conquor.

Both the Confederate and the Union army are having built what is called gun boats for the navigation of the Mis. They are made low, and are covered over with half inch wrought iron riveted on verry securely, and will prove a verry formidable boat in their way and will be capable of resisting cannon balls. Numbers of these boats are on the way of completion.

These Boats are to be used as conveys to transporting of army stores, as well as battering down forts that may be on the rivers. They carry several heavy guns.

The Confederates has had for some time past a pretty strong force in the mountains of Virginia at a place called Cumberland Gap. These forces are in the command of Genl. George Crittendon and Zollicoffee. This place is the key or pass-way through the mountains, and by holding this part of the mountains would prevent any reinforcements from the west to the union army in Virginia.

The Federals, aware of this, were determined to open the way if possible through to eastern Virginia. So along toward the middle of this month they start off with a heavy force in that direction to attact the confederates that were occupying the gap.

They met at a small stream, called Fishing Creek. The confederates were rather under a surprise. The battle commenced in a vigorous manner by both sides. The fight lasted for some time, and it, being at the time, foggy weather that both partys became a little mixed up. Genl. Zollicoffee mistaking a regiment of the enemy for his own rode up to them for the purpose of encouraging his men as he thought. He was among them before he made the discovery. He was ordered to surrender. This he refused, but dispatched his opponent. The next moment he was pierced with several shots, dying a brave man.

This threw the confederate forces into a confusion, and it was impossible to get order restored again. The union forces, pressing on the advantage they had, compelled the confederate to fall back and retreat.

Genl. George Crittenden managed to get the army off after sustaining a defeat. The losses was said to be large on both sides, and the loss of Zollicoffee may be said to be a serious one to the confederate army.

Genl. George Crittenden was senior in command and tis said had the matter been entrusted to Zollicoffee to command that the fate of the day would have been different from what it was. Genl C. kept his capper heated all the time, which made him incapable to command. **Life is too valuable to be trusted with a whiskeyhead.**

Up to the Battle of Fishing Creek the Confederate army had the assendency in victories, and to all appearance was going on in a prosperous way. But by this time the Federal army had increased its forces largely and were in a condition to prosecute the War in a more vigorous manner, which they set about immediately. The first demonstration was on a small fort, called Fort Henry, which is situated on the Ten. River, built by the confederates.

This fort is on rather low ground for high water, situated not far from the mouth of the river. Unfortunately, for the confederates at the time the attact was made by the Federals the waters was quite swolen, so much so, that they could scarcely remain in the fort. Could make but little resistance in the way of a fight—so it required but little tact to capture the place. In fact, there was but little resistance offered on the part of the Confederates, and they abandoned it to the enemy.

This thing, happening almost immediately after the Fishing Creek affair, gave the Federals encouragement. They felt flushed with victory.

The confederate forces that was at this fort made their way across the country to Fort Donalson which is situated on the Cumberland River some distance below Nashville, Ten. This takes place along in the first days of Feb. 1862.

February 1, 1862

The armies in Virginia and round the borders of the Southern states were having frequent heavy skirmishes with each other. Some hot contests would frequently ensue. Out side of this, nothing worthy of note, since the great Battle of Manassas.

Notwithstanding, matters look a little gloomy for the Confederate cause, nothing to look to for help but the **Great Author** of mans destinies, and a determination and perseverence to go through with the undertaking at all hazzards.

Though there is gloom, active preparation is still progressing with both armies.

The western waters at this time were in good Boating condition, and each of the contending parties had got a number of Iron clad Gun boats built and a float. They were plying them pretty effectually against each other.

Battle at Fort Donaldson

Immediately after the Surrender of Fort Henry active preparation was made by the Federals to make an attact on Fort Donaldson. They lost no time in making the attempt. The confederate considered themselves pretty strongly fortified and could resist almost any force that could be brought against them at that time, having massed a heavy force.

February 10, 1862

By February 10, 1862 the Federals begin to make their appearance in large force for the purpose of an attact on the Fort. In a short time their numbers had increased to quite a large body of men. They had also numbers of gun boats to assist in the attact. All things being now ready, skirmishing commenced by both parties and at times became pretty general.

There was at this time a heavy snow on the ground wet, and freezing. The confederate had formed their line of battle, occupying their ditches and earth works. About the 12th a general engagement commenced and continued for about three days of hard fighting. The confederate remaining during the whole time in their ditches, in mud, and water. Scarcely taking the time to eat, and sleeping on their arms during the night. They were now fighting against superior men. The Federals still reinforceing all the time, they having enough men to relieve those that were in the engagement.

The Confederates after having fought hard for three days, no reinforcements comeing to their relief, they, hungry, fatigued, and worn out, could stand no longer and had finally to give way and surrender the place to the Federal army. Camp equipage &c.

A large number of men made prisoners. Also officers of all grades and among that number was our townsman Coln. J.B. Palmer.

The surrender, of the Fort and men devolved upon Gen Buckner, being the jr in command. He was made prisoner with the others—those that could get off did so.

The killed and wounded was said to have been heavy on both sides and a desperately hard fought battle.

There was some lack of judgement. The confederate had got too much of the idea that they could whip three Yankees to one. They did not take into count that, they were fighting against western men who, were as familiar with fire arms as themselves and many more so. It is said that the question was asked of the commanding Gen. "Would he need any assistance?" His reply of this manner, "I can stand any force that may come."

Gen. Sidney Johnson was occupying Bolinggreen, Ky. at this time. His position thought now to be of little service. He orders an evacuation of the place, moves what stores he is able and orders the balance to be destroyed. Starts his troops on the road to Nashville. Genl. Buell is on the road not far behind him with a heavy force of men. In fact, is somewhat pressing for as Johnsons rear guard is leaving Bolinggreen that of Buell is just making its apperance.

Fall of Fort Donaldson

When the news of the fall of Donaldson reached Nashville every thing was thrown into confusion. The public stores were thrown open and wasted goods and provisions were thrown in the streets pel mel. Every body at liberty to help themselves as best suited. Bacon, Sugar, coffee, Blankets, shoes, and clothing, generally. In fact, there was neither head or tail in the matter. No one appeared to take any particular interest in how things were disposed of. Such was the confusion among the people.

Many were leaving their houses, procuring conveyances and moving off to some other part, leaving the house hold to the mercy of the enemy and robbers. The commissaries sent off what stores they could through the general confusion.

This news reached Nashville on Sunday. Some time, about the middle of the day, the people were at church, as usual, but, when the news came here was another great stir. All was on the move. No one felt disposed to assist in singing the doxology. Matters was concluded in short order. It was who shall get out of the church first, not much respect was paid to fancy Bonnets and costly dresses. The Parsons standing, looking with astonishment, start after the retreating parties into the streets and are lost in the general confusion. It was like the fall of Jerico, enacted on a small scale.

However the Yankees did not reach Nashville for four days after the disaster at Donaldson. They came quietly, but cautiously, feeling their way like a blind man, not knowing where the danger might lay. They are brave, that is some of them, and they have a great horrow of being shot.

They finally reached Nashville safely without much trouble on their part and took formal possession of the place, which is to say, this is **ours**. After feeling round and became satisfied that there was no danger brought the men to a halt and stacked arms. A general forage now commences with the soldiers. They appear as hungry as hyenas after a hard winter. Almost every house was visited in search of something to eat.

Things now assumed a **Blue** appearance and was rather chilling to the feelings.

February 15, 1862

In the mean time, Genl. Johnson had fallen back as far as Murfreesboro with the confederate troops, after having heavy and fatigueing marches.

The soldiers looked jaded and worn out, it having rained quite heavy during their march to this place. They were wet and hungry. But with all, they put on a cherful countinance. As it was intended to make some stay at this place they set about immediately to pitching their tents and put things in order. In a fiew days they had got themselves in a condition to look comfortable and satisfied.

As it was necessary to make some change in army arrangement, a reconstructing was immediately commenced by the Genl and officers. After this, it was intended to proceed to some point further south. The troops by this time had rested, and every thing had been put in order.

It was now determined by Genl. Johnson to take up the line of march. After having remained at this place about two weeks they leave at this date.

The R. Road was put in requisition for the transportation of troops, guns, and amunition, and the destination is said to be Corrinth, Missipi. After the start was made, it was but a short time before all were off.

Our town was quietly reposing, not dreaming that an army would tread our quiet streets, or that we should have any thing to molest us in our every day avocation. But, merely to speak of war as a thing that was raging in other parts of the country and not likely to ever reach us—these and similar feelings were in the minds of all.

When one morning, early, our ears is greeted by the sound of the horses hoof, the roll of Artillery wagons and trains, the heavy tread of the retreating soldier and cavalry in our midst. If dreaming, we are now awakened to a new sense of feeling, that war is spreading its baneful effects through the land and its future effects to be dreaded.

About this time, a man by name John H. Morgan makes his appearance. He is commanding a company of cavalry of some fifty men. He is a man of great energy, and it seems has made his mark where ever he has gone, a Kentuckian by birth. He remained at this place some days after Gen. Johnson left. His operations has been mostly through Kentucky, destroying bridges and tearing up R. Roads, which has created a deadly hate by the federal soldiers against him. We shall likely hear more from him in future with respect to his doings in the army.

My son, W.I.S.—Impressed with the feelings of duty he owed his country, volunteered his servisis as a soldier and joined Morgan in the cavalry sirvece-for weal or woe.

February 20, 1862

Nothing of importance appears to be on hand on February 20, 1862. All is quiet again, the soldiers having all left this place. The people are satisfied that such is the case, not that they were of any particular annoyance, but that they prefered quiet to the confusion that occurred of necissity.

Can hear of nothing of the army in Virginia that is unusual. All are quiet there and at other points.

Thus, it will be seen, we are to ourselves again. The carpenter plying the hammer, the Blaksmith his anvil, the merchant and his costomers bargaining over the sale of goods. The farmer is making arrangement for his future crop. All is life and animation. The report is that the Yankee cavalry is making some visits every day or so in the neighborhood for purposes not satisfactory to all parties. They are comeing up the Nashville pike more frequently and returning again.

Reports of what is seen by this one and that. Things begins to look like some trouble is brewing in this quarter. Every trip they make up the road, nearer approaches is made.

March 10, 1862

The Yankees finally ventured into Murfreesboro headed by Genl. Mitchell with a heavy force cavalry. They rode round the public square and halted oposite a croud of citizens who had gathered about at the approach of the troops. The Genl., straitning himself up, and in a pompus manner, addresses the citizens some what in this style.—I am master of this place! And then goes on to say how he wishes matters to be understood and what he intends doing. His object was to restore the union, law, and order.

It appears the Rail Road and Bridges was burned by the Confederate army on their retreat from this place and Nashville. In fact, there was but fiew bridges on any road escaped destruction.

During his remarks, he puts the question to the croud of citzens who were present to know if the burning was done with the consent and wish of the people of this place. Some one spoke and remarked that it might or not, could not well answer the question—another person said it **was** done with the consent of the people. The Genl. replys, if that be the case he knew what sort of people he had to deal with. Acordingly—after making a short stay, they returned to Nashville.

This is our first introduction to Yankee soldiers and small specimen of their politeness. On their first entrance in town, every man had his thumb on the cock of his gun. Rode round in this manner until they saw the citizens were a peaceable people instead of a savage race, as they may have thought. They made a neat appearance as soldiers. Their uniforms were all regular, and dress, of sky blue.

No person appeared to have the least alarm as to their visit. Thought it would be only a temporary thing. That if they did come, they would pass off again in the course of a fiew days and things would move on as usual.

About three days after the cavalry visit to this place, our ears are greeted with the sound of drum and fife and the rattle of artillery wagons and colums of infantry advancing—colours flying—every thing appeared to be on the move. Our peaceble town again thrown into excitement—now, by an army of invasion. They come and take formal possession of the place and hoist the flag of the U.S. instead of the Confederate which was on the court house steeple. They set to pitching their camps, which was pretty much all round the town, convenint to water.

March 15, 1862

Genl. Mitchell has arrived with his whole command. Takes controle of things in and about the place. After he had got his army pretty well settled, commences regulating things for the people. He establishes a provost marshal whose duty is to administer oaths and give military passes to the citizens. This officer is the personage of one O.C. Rounds.

Among other things the Genl. undertakes the repair of the R. Road and Bridges to Nashville, having a great many mechanices in his army and all the necessary tools at hand. He is not long in getting the road in running order. All army stores and provisions up to this time had to be transported by wagon trains from Nashville.

He thought it was necessary to make a miltary Gov. among his other regulations. Col. Parkhurst was appointed and duly inaugurated and commenced his administration. His teritory of government was small, but he felt the importance of his position. The reigns began to tighten. The people felt somewhat cramped in their freedom but was still disposed to feel and act in an independant manner.

Goods had became scarce, but all the business houses were as usual trading on what they had on hand. All, in a manner, had sold out.

Gen. S. Johnson had fallen back to Corinth, Miss. and commenced the work of fortifying his position at this place. Island No. 10, on the Miss. River, was still in possession of the confederate army at this time, but strong movements were about being made by the federal army to take it.

There's considerable murmuring among the soldiers of Gen. Johnson for his move so far south, but from all appearances it was the best thing that could be done at the time. His army had been so much disorganized by the battle at Fort Donaldson, his losses having been great in the killed, wounded, and large number of prisoners which had been surrendered by the movement. He had an opportunity to reconstruct and put every thing in a proper condition for future operation.

Gen. Mitchell, having completed the R. Road and bridges, started the cars running to Nashville. All other matters pertaining to army arrangements feels now in a condition to make a further south movement. After having detatched about fifteen hundred of his men to hold the post at Murfreesboro, he with the main force takes up the line of march on his way to Huntsville, Alabama. In this move he had no difficulty more than to march along. True there was a small force at that place of confederate soldiers, but the capture was easy.

The Gen. was not altogether well pleased with the inhabitance of this community for the reason they did not shew a disposition to honor his calling nor that friendship he was entitled to. No invitations to dinners or fine suppers was tendered to him. All this caused the Genl. to have very little sympathy for the people and at times they thought he was disposed to be a little hard on them.

Well! This is war! Hatred appears the dominant passion now. All the finer feelings are being blinded. As has been remarked, the Gen. is on his way south, where he may find things more genial to his feelings. He is putting down the rebellion. He arrives at Huntsville without much difficulty, takes formal possession, hoists a flag at some convenient place. "I have seen, I have conquered." One of the fortunate Genls who captured without seeing the enemy.

He does things up pretty much at Huntsville as he did at Murfreesboro. Established himself here, possibly fearing there might be danger in going further west. Sends a force along the R. Road and orders a fiew bridges to be **burned**, which is now a legitimate thing on his part, but quite a chrime when done by the confederate.

A blockade is commenced at the Huntsville depot and finished so that the cars can pass through—supposed to be for storage of cotton.

The Gen., having established himself, the next thing was to look after the loyalty of the people of the country. The next thing that attracts the attention is cotton. Such a thing as confiscation had been introduced. When a man was found that had a good lot cotton, he was generally elected disloyal and of course he had to hand over the article to the order of the Gen. and perhaps to undergo an imprisonment.

It is said the thing was managed in this way. Now Mitchell had a soninlaw with him in the army. Cotton is confiscated and sold by order of the Gen. and this soninlaw, who is a partner, being purchaser, ships the cotton North and sold. A lively business was carried on in this way.

This thing at last appeared to look too glaring to the civilized world. So, the powers that be at Washington had to send for the Gen. and papers and go through a partial trial, but as to the results of the investigation it matters not.

In the mean time his men were not idle speculators of things. They too wish to reap some of the benefits. The harvest is ripe, and they throw in the sickle.

These men were over the country, getting up or stealing what they can lay hands on. Horses was a common property, and then there was what was called orders for searching citizen's houses and farms, as they say, for guns and amunition. This is sufficent licence. They go to any mans house to make search; require them to open drawers, chests, and take what suits. If the man is thought to have too much money, they make convenint to make a night search for that. Call for meals from the citizens and after they had eaten would get up and leave with scarcely a thank you, gather the pottry that might be about the yard and any thing else that they may want. By way of amusement, set fire to a house to see it burn. Such is a sketch of Gen. Mitchells army in and about Huntsville. Space is not sufficint to detail the one-tenth part of the meanness of these devils in the abolitionist army.

And at the same time they were poisoning the minds of the negros, persuaiding them to leave home and go with them to the camps, which they willingly accepted the offer.

April 15, 1862

The Federal armies now has the ascendency. Every thing now appears to favor their movements. They have made a demonstration on Island No. 10, and after some resistance they capture it and take full possession.

Not long after, a gun Boat fight takes place near Memphis between the Confederates and Federals, the latter make short work by capturing all the boats but one. It makes an escape down the river to Vicksburg.

The Federal formally take Memphis which will prove to be a point of importance to them and a great annoyance to the confederacy by the loss, being a good base for army supplies.

New Orleans

New Orleans was surrendered without much trouble on the part of the Yankees. It was supposed that the rebels would have withstood a considerable resistance before they would have given up the place, being a key to their operations. But it seems in this case a demand was in a manner sufficint—as matters are going looks any thing but satisfactory to the people. Now feel if the thing was to be done over, that it would cost old Abe a little more powder and lead to purchase the city and a fiew of his boys thrown in to the bargan.

May as well here give a reason—Gen. Butler is now the commander. From the times he has been here, he is disposed to make all feel his power and bend to his will. Orders arrests of persons and appropriates property to his own use, sends persons to prison, charges them of being disloyal to the U. States government. To conclude, he is disposed to be a **Tyrant**. No crowned head of Europe can do worse than he has done so far as he has gone. He is a General by title, but not a brave man. No brave man will condescend to do as small mean things as Butler has done in N. Orleans. From the time he has been there, has the power and makes use of it. A **dictator**, his word is the law—or rather makes so. It is almost impossible to use words that would express a contempt for such a man. Time will develop his character; history may speak of him as a monster when his actions are more generally known.

Vicksburg

The next place a call is made at Vicksburg by the Federal forces. A demand of the Mayor of this place is made to surrender the city. Replys to this effect, "Come and take it." At the writing of this it is not taken—**Hard nut to crack.**

At Corinth, April 25, 1862

The last mention, the confederate army was at Corinth making arrangements for the accommodations of the sick, and wounded soldiers, constructing tents, and doing other necessary work for the comefort of the well portion of the army. In a short time, things had became pretty well settled. The soldiers had got quarters in order, having constructed hospitals and put the sick and wounded under treatment. Placed out picket guards for the safety of the place. Also, the fortifications are undergoing an improvement. Every thing in this way was active.

In the mean time, the Yankees had commenced their march in the direction of Corinth, but in a slow and cautious manner. They cut timber, threw up levies, and causewayed their roads all the way through the swamps. This was necessary as the roads ran through low bottom lands and had been cut up so much by the confederate army in the retreat through, that no passage could be made without this precaution. Their bagage, being so much more cumbersom than that of the rebels, they generally travel with double the quantity—their wagons are heavy, substantial, well calculated, for the purpose.

However, they make a good road to the high lands and continue to make advances with their whole army.

They commence a seris of rifle pits, pretty much the whole way to Corinth, worked their men hard at this kind of business. The picket guards, having slight skirmishing all the time. This work was progressing, which took several weeks to work through to Corinth.

Genl. Bureguard remained at Corinth with his army until the Federals were near enough for him to throw balls in their camps. Their last rifle pits was this distanced. He now concludes to move his army on further south. He commenced the movement in a quiet manner—sending off all the wounded and sick. On board of the cars, amunition and provision. In this way in the course of four days had nearly every thing that was worth moving off. Keeping up the appearance by a fiew men that he was making preparation to receive the enemy. The enemy moving forward in a slow cautious manner to make an attact on the encampment.

Gen Bureguard played off a little strategy in this case. He had a number of pine logs made the proper size for cannon and placed on his breast works to represent cannon with the ends blackened. Some of them quite large diameter—and to carry out the figure had stakes placed and fixed off with old "Sesesh" pants, old coat and cap to match. A musket to each of these "so called" men. Thus made, a number was placed about these formidable cannon as picket guards. It had the desired effect. The enemy were held in check at least a day longer than they would have been; however, they continued to advance and occaisionally thrown over a shell as a feeler. But these "Sesesh" was't afraid of the shells. They stood ground, made no replys to the enemy. At last, a fiew that was more resolute thought to reconoiter. Came to the conclusion that they might venture to storm the fort.

After a consultation it was agreed, that they would make a charge. The word is given, and a "gallant charge" is made right into the rebel fortifications. Regardless of the pickets that stood their ground, what was their surprise and mortification, when it was ascertained they had **gone two days ago**—the **guards** were of course "arrested" for the deception they played off.

However the town was captured and formal possession was taken of it and the fortification.

An old livery stable, being the largest building in the place a flag staff was formally naild to the gable, and the stars and stripes was thrown to the breese. The remainder of the army now arrive in full force and things begin to assume a new face.

Thus, the tale is told, but cannot vouch for the truth of the whole of it. A part may be true. It remains for future historians to say.

Corinth Taken, April 30, 1862

Corinth and fortifications, being now in full possession of the Federal army, the point they were contending for. The next thing to be done was to set down and write out a full report of the battle and taking of Corinth. The same published in the northern papers. But, really did not exactly know which way the enemy had gone—whether up the road or down. For not one **word** could they get out of the "**Sesesh**" **pickets** that was captured. It was finally concluded to send a force of cavalry on each end of the road and ascertain which way Bureguard had gone with his army. Accordingly, rations was prepared and men mounted, set out on their mission after beating about for two or three days. The party that had taken down end of the road came suddenly to the picket guard. There they found the "Sesesh" sure enough, occupying a place called Tupaloe, Miss. in rather an unhealthy place to follow them.

They came back and finished up the report, "We persued the enemy several miles. They threw down their guns, nap sacks, blankets, and scattered things generally along the road and skedadled in general quick time. We lost in this skirmish not one man. The enemy lost a great many more." All now in camps. Hostilities now, for a time, suspended.

It was now getting late in the spring of the year. The Yankees occupying Corinth and the rebel army at Tupaloe, Mi. Each content to remain quiet for a time, attending to the comefort of their sick and wounded soldiers.

The water of this section of country was not very favorable to the health of either army which caused numbers to be placed on the sick list. With this exception, things about the camps are quiet. Hear of no moves in any other is being made to cause any sensation.

Will now leave the respective armys for a time. Each are fortifying their positions and until a move of some kind is made, shall look to some other quarter for an item.

And here it is—This should have come to notice some time since. Being overlooked the presumption is it will do at the present time. The scene took place during the summer of 1861. Events change so fast that it is hard to keep the mind on all that happens.

War in a Tea Pot

It will be remembered the subject of war was in the minds and mouths of all the people through the land. They had been fully aroused. Old Tennessee was rolling and tumbling under the pain of secession.

Her sons were buckling on their armour and, fearlessly rushing to war. It bethought the worthy Boro'ans to put themselves in a definsive attitude, having determined on war to the **knife, and knife to the handle**, against the vandal invaders of our soil. Hence, a call is made to rally to the standard to defend their rights, their liberties, and their hearth stones.

A regiment of valiant men is formed in short order called, **The Home Guards** of Murfreesboro. Officers are appointed as this was no time to trifle and stump speaking. It was a case of emergency.

The aspirants—Sam. Winston, who felt himself competent as Gen. commander of the volunteer forces. Jno. W. Childress, capt.; Jno. Leiper Lick; Ivy Haines, sargent, and Wm. Ransom, com. to the army. Thus officered the next thing was to equip. Gen. Winston orders each to bring his shot gun or rifle, and be promp.

A day is appointed for parade and go through the exercise. It would have filled Wellington's heart with pride to have possessed such a band of patriots as marched out to the city commons the first day—defenders!!!

Well, they arrive at the shade. The capt. takes them through a thorough course of shoulder arms, order arms, present arms, load, and motion of firing all of which was gone through satisfactorily. The Gen. and his staff on horse back watching the movements with pride and satisfaction with the thought that Old Abe's minnions would not dare to put foot on our soil while such a band of patriots were under arms. The country is safe.

Under this flow of feeling, the Gen. assumes to take command to go through a fiew manoevers as a kind of flourish.

Now, Gentlemen! You will preceive we will go the motion of forming a **holler** square. I want you to take particular notice. This is to keep off cavalry! The company now being in a line. Attention! Home Guards, Right Wheel! The whole commence moving. Stop, gentlemen, don't mean all! Some to stop here. Right Wheel! Again—Right Wheel—Right Wheel. Now this is what is called a holler square. You preceive how you can shoot all round.

That was well done gentlemen—I thank you for your attention. Gen. Smith will take you through the balance of the manoevers. Resigns command. It will be seen he is well qualified to fill the office of commander.

Gen. Smith, being on foot and an old hand at militia drilling, takes charge. Forms lines, counter marches—Plattoons—Sections—and, finally, the company into two divisions-and fights a regular (sham) pitch battle. These divisions are separated; go through the motion of loading, and firing—charge, bayonets! This motion is done by one division passing through the other and recharge back, (unlike the present mode of fighting). Partys a distance apart. The charging party advances. The other run - they in turn, charge—another run.

The Home guards return.

The most remarkable feature of the affair was our sargent, Haines. He, being a counterpart of Fallstaff, supporting a long, broad sword, draging on the ground, the butt lengthened out by a tow string to make ends meet.

The sword may once have been Gen. Marion or Genl. Greens or other renowned gen. of old—from appearance. Great drops of sweat rolling down his cheeks like tears, shed for his beloved countrys flag.

The balance of the officers, bearing a conspicous part, feeling the weight of government on their shoulders. But, none felt so forcibly as did Sargent Haines, on this occaision. It would seem there was "Glory enough, for one day." But, not so, more was to be done yet before the end. The patriotism of the Sargent was in a flame in his bosom. He was destined to be delivered.

Raising the Confederate Flag

After the flag was raised and considered a fixed fact, the people were looking for some demonstration on the occaision. Sargent Haines, being present, was loudly called on by all for a speech. He advances like **Fallstaff**, mounts the rostrum. But, unlike **Cicero**, delivers himself as follows:

Feller Citizens!!

These are times of danger and peril in which we all live. The storm is no longer in the distance. But, is already upon us and the situation demands that every man take his position. **Mine** has **long been fixed**— cheers. The sargent here rises on tip toe. Forty five years I have lived under the Stars and Stripes. The last ten or fifteen have been one continued encroachment of the North on the inhabitants of the south. Our remonstrances have availed us nothing. We must be the protectors and defenders of our own section. The balance of **my** days be they many or fiew, I am willing to devote in defence of my country. Cheers!

When I contemplate the wrongs perpetrated, and the indignations heaped on the south, it makes my verry! **Blood Boil** in my vains, and my whole nature calls for vengence on the perfidious Yankee nation. Cheers!

I am no speaker as you all know. But times like these require that **every man** should be able to give a reason for his action and to place himself beyond impeachment on the **record**—long, and loud cheering.

Simon Sickles, a Dutch jew merchant, was next called to the stand. Said, "I cannot speak de English so goot as my neighbor vat is chost been speaking. But dat flag ish my flag, and I follows dat flag to de bitter end. Loud cheering.

Many others were called on and responded during the evening. Some even quite eloquent; others were cautious and modest. They approached the subject like a boy walking on a pond of very thin ice.

And then, there was an under current of patriotism among those who did not make speeches, but went about talking to small crouds. Manifested the highest degree of liberality on the occaision, willing to give away any amount of means of others?! As per example, W.C. Duffer.

W.C. Duffer

He did not make a speech from the stand as did the gallant Sargent. He said, "I have plenty in my store, widows and the wives of the volunteers can have!" When application is made for a little coffee by a widow, he **charges** twenty five pr ct more than the market price, because the article is getting scarce and rising. But, **subscriber** $125—for the **cause.**

But, William! goes a long the streets of Murfreesboro inciting the populace to acts of violence. Spencer has a large lot of Sack Salt, and Collards, a quantity of flour on hand. Says, "**They ought** to go to any of the grocery houses and get what they want; **I will** see them out in a law suit to my **last bottom dollar!**"

Again says he, "I am willing to equip **Twenty Volunteers** at my own expense." And at an other time, "I will starve and let my family suffer before I will submit to the **Lincoln Role**—(Barclay)." Subscribes 125 - to the cause.

Here is patriotism that will put the Devil to blush, if his magesty has any shame.

Such is a birds eye-view of the times. About this date, it would take a volume to note all that was said and done by individuals at these times. That would look ridiculous in their own eyes.

Buoya, or Butcher Knife

There was quite a business among the volunteers having made a large knife called a Buoya or Butcher Knife, about twenty inches long and about two wide in the blade. Would weigh when finished about two pounds. This was a part of the soldiers equipage, beside his gun and other articles, made to cut the Yankees head and arms off in a fight.

May 10, 1862

The people had become reconciled to their situation and moving on with their business in the usual way with the exception did not feel quite so free on account of having to procure passes to go out. To get that, an oath had to be administered. One that had been manufactured for the occaision by the pvst. marshal. True there were not so many came to town as would have if the matter of oath had been let alone.

Sometimes, a negro would be induced to leave home and go to the camps. In this case, the master would follow up to get his property. In that case, he would have to swallow a bit of an oath, that is, taking oath of allegience to the United States, for all had sined and come short of the glory of Lincoln.

However to make the matter short—it was thought to give all a chance to repent and confess their sins and be accepable among the nations. Gov. Johnson makes an appointment, assisted by E. Cooper, whose business is to exhort the people to return from their sins and be accepable union men in the sight of Abraham.

The day arrived for the meeting. An order was issued saying all may come to town on that day free of passes and hear the word, as it is, in Johnson. A Flag was prepared for the occaision and hoisted on the pinacle of the court house. Cannon was fired on the public square, and a flourish or two by the Brass band.

The Gov. now advances toward the stand, mounts the rostrum, and looking over the crowds in a dignified manner commences letting off in his old peculiar Democratic style in days of yore. He spoke about two hours when he gave way to Mr Cooper who was verry pursuasive in his arguments and reasonings. He continued to entertain the people about one hour and a half.

When the doors were opened for the reception of members, there were about five joined and a large number on the bench, undetermined what to do. Just at this time, there is a fine opening for a revival if the proper course would be taken with the people. All they need is good treatment and encouragement, take off restraints in the place of adding on, meddle not with their negros, horses, or property of any kind, further than army necessity requires. If this course should be pursued, Tennesse will all be right in a short time.

May 20, 1862

By May 20, 1862 there is but little of importance going on in the armys. The Federal army have pretty much the possession of the west end of the state of Tennessee. Their cavalry range over that portion, committing many depradations upon the citizens, taking off negros, and horses, and property generally.

Have accumulated a large number of negros at Cairo at the mouth of the Ohio River. Many had run off from home and others had been forced off from their masters. Tis hard to understand why this is done. They say that they are not abolitionist, did not come to fight for the negro. When such a thing is intimated to them, spurn the idea.

However the thing is done, and numbers care verry little whether it is right or wrong. Done, as a matter of annoyance, to the people whom they look upon as a proud, aristocratic race and above taking notice of poor **folks** like these.

Occaisionally, can hear of cavalry skirmishes in different quarters, but generally turns out a small matter as in these encounters. The parties can see the strength of its opponent, and the smallest makes a **gallant** man get out of the way. Suppose, this is what is called **fighting** their way out against great odds. Did not loose a man. Soldiers have a way of playing off.

May 25, 1862

Coln. Parkhurst, who is military gov. of the Town, issues an order on May 25, 1862 that all persons engaged in any business must take the oath of allegience to the U.S. under pain of having their business houses closed. None could do business without thus complying. This was one turn on the screw to tighten matters up a little. There were but very fiew at this time attempting to do, and if they had nothing to do business on, the goods all sold out.

But, the oath. This was a thing no one had any relish for, no matter what his feelings might be, and the more it was talked about the more the people became opposed. Felt like a tresspas on on their feelings. It was simple enough in its nature. All a man had to do was to go before Capt. Rounds, hold up the hand until he could repeat or read to applicant the oath, and at the end so help me, God, was added. The contents was varied to suit the times. A pass is now given which you carry in your pocket as a **free man**. None now to molest or make afraid. Name set down in book. Taken the oath.

The people did not croud the pro marshal very much for the gracious favor. Consequently, had quite an easy time in his office—an hour or so during the day—then, ride for health.

It became necessary to have the **corporation** take the oath. That is the Mayor and Aldermen, so thought the Gov. and Pro. They were doing business in an illegal way, and for that reason must take a **swear**. Here a difficulty arose about the matter among the aldermen. They could not reconcile it to their feelings, as several of them had sons in the confederate army. On this ground were opposed to the oath, and the sympathy of the whole board was for the south. The thing stood several days undetermined. How to dispose of it.

However, after a time, some changes being made in the board of Aldermen and for the sake of peace and interest of the public, they submitted to take the oath as Mayor and Aldermen of the City of Murfreesboro. But, whether that oath also applyed individually or not, will be left for the future to determine.

It will now be seen that things as regards the functions of Mayor and Aldermen is in motion again. Goes on appearantly well for a time.

But, it is soon found clashing with the military. They assuming more authority than justly belong to them, being the stronger party would carry their point. The aldermen, seeing this, they finally became more slack in their exertion to do any thing—so the matter died out.

Incident

During Genl. Mitchell's stay in Murfreesboro, he, wishing to have a conference with the mayor on some business, sends word or asks when the mayor can be found. The Mayor understanding the wish, and not disposed to have any meeting with the Genl. being one of those determined sort of men, makes up his mind to go fishing and let him wait his time.

As he leaves with his poles on his shoulder, remarks "If Genl. Mitchell wishes to see me more than I do him, he can come where I am fishing. I shall not go to him."

June 1, 1862
Colnn Parkhurst's Campaign to Chatanooga

On June 1, 1862 Coln. Parkhurst took the notion that he would make a campaign in search of "Sesesh." Chatanooga was his point of destination. His men is fitted out with the necessary rations for the trip.

Starts out in the direction of Mc Minnville and by way of Sparta over the mountains. Like Bonapart crossing the alps, but instead of being in the winter was in the month of June. His men, fatigued, and nearly woarn out and in no plight for fighting, if there should be any, to do.

They finally arrive in sight of the place on the oposite side of the river. They slip near the bank in breathless expectation that something is about to be done. The nearest object to them was an old Tobacco warehouse. Thought they could see almost an army of soldiers moving about.

However, they formed a line of battle on the margin of the river. Discharges two or three vollies of musketry across the stream at the said warehouse. They receive no response to this demonstration.

A little consultation is held, and the conclusion is a trap laid to draw them over the river and overpower and finally capture their forces. The coln. had too much inteligence to be caught in this manner. He reconoiters to find out the "Sesesh" if possible and their probable strength.

It turns out, there were a small force of the "Sesesh" in and about Chatanooga. Stationed they had been watching the movements of the gallant Col. and command. They did not appear to be alarmed at the firing, having the river between them. However, a portion shewed themselves.

Matters began to assume a different appearance to what was first expected. The Col., now satisfied that his first conclusions were correct as to strength, and orders were given to pull up, strike and retreat. They were persued a short distance by the enemy but were unable to come up, if it was the wish. As the order was double quick, down hill.

In this attact on Chatanooga no body was hurt, the thing having been so well managed.

The Coln., after a fatigueing march, returns again safely to Murfreesboro, having been out about fifteen days in this campaign. This feat was performed by the 9th Michigan and the first battle they had fought. The achievements will make a bright page in history.

The soldiers had many incidences to relate, of what they did and what happened on their march. Of the amusement they had. How they annoyed the old "Sesesh" Women, capturing their Turkeys and chickens, and other petty depradations on the way.

As a matter of history, it may be well to speak of an incident that took place during the later compeign to Chatanooga. It appears on the return of Col. P., he captures a confederate flag on the road that some playful boys had placed on their mammas **hen house** for their own amusement. This was a rare **Trophy**, but cost little to make the capture. The boys of course made objections. It availed nothing; had to submit to the loss. It was brought to Murfreesboro. A novel scene takes place on the arrival of the union men, a display that rivals any thing in the annals of history.

The men are formed in line on horse back. The Col. places himself at the head of the column. The Confederate Flag has a long string attached to it, the other end of string is fastened to his horse's tail so it will drag along on the ground. All things being ready to make the start from the R. Depot. The word March! is given. The whole column move off. The Col. in the lead, with the flag wallowing in the dust fastened to his horse tail. They make their way to the public square, and pass round in this **dignified manner**, cheering as they go, assisted by the little boys and negros. Genl. Jackson would say "Glory enough for one day."

From this, very little is heard, particular of this Coln. except as a gallant at **parties** of this **First Class Citizens**, which is quite common at this time.

June 10, 1862

On June 10, 1862 there was nothing at this time to attract any particular interest among the citizens. Scarcely any business that could be done so the time was idled away by them.

The Military were on parade every day. Officers on horse back prancing about the streets. The men all in regular neat uniform of a sky blue. Their guns and amunition well arranged. Then there was a great display of flags and banners belonging to the different companys, and there were a profusion of drummers and fifers. When they started out was like bedlam let loose, with the keen shriek of the fife and the dreadful rattle of drums. The union to be restored by display.

About this time we hear of a man by name of **Forrest** making his way round by the mountains near Chatanooga. He is from Mississippi. Command a cavalry force of about one thousand men. His rank is that of Col. Makes his appearance at Mc Minnville, Ten., and establishes head quarters at and around through the county. Remains here some length of time. Watching the movements of the federal forces that was stationed at this place.

His scouting partys extended their trips almost in sight of town, but went about in such way that they did not excite much suspicion as to what their business was in the neighborhood.

There were stationed at this post about fifteen hundred men, and a battery of six cannon. These were kept as a provost guard to hold Murfreesboro, and keep things in order. It was this lot of Yankees that Forrest was keeping a careful watch over and was interested for their sake and welfare.

The Federals were getting somewhat careless as to the danger that threatened them, having heard so often reports of the "Sesesh" being in the country. They did not believe it. For the reason they never came across them in their travels. Concluded that it must all be a "Sesesh" lie and on that ground made them selves easy.

Disagreement, between Cols. Parkhurst & Lester

From some cause, not necessary to know, a misunderstanding of serious character takes place between these two distinguished characters, Colns. Parkhurst and Lester. The latter saw proper to move his encampment (which had been in connection with P.), on Stones River about two miles from Murfreesboro. Parkhurst remained at the old place at Maneys Springs about half-mile from town. Then there was a portion of said command which makes a third division. They were occupying the court house and city hotel.

It is now seen how the force is divided. Capt. Hewit, who commands the six gun battery, is stationed on the river with Lester.

Every thing now moving on in an easy manner verry little to do. More to eat and amuse themselves at ball or playing marbles in the streets during the day, and at night will not hesitate to lift a hen off her quiet roost. As a matter of seasoning take a fiew onions out of gardens along. Ease the concience by saying he is an old "Sesesh," any how.

They are quite sassy when in conversation about Sesesh soldiers. Shew a disposition to come up with them and have a fight, but it appears have caution enough **not** to come as two generally play at the same game.

Forageing was going on intensively. Almost every day long trains would start out in the morning with eight or ten armed men to each wagon. In the evening, returns, heavy loaded with corn, fodder, oats, and hay, and garnished with a good supply of poltry of all kinds and, other articles of eatables. Any thing they wanted was taken. This is what they called, subsisting on the enemy. Sometimes they would pretend to give a receipt for corn of about three or four barrels to the wagon, when it would have double the amounts and fodder in proportion. The applicant for pay could scarcely ever find the comisary, and if he did was refered to some other person. If found a receipt given to be paid, if the **man proved** to be a **good union man** at the end of the war. That of **course** would be **done**. In all these cases the comissary pocketed the proceeds, and Uncle Sam had to foot the bill, and "Sesesh" had to go with his finger in his mouth or some other convenient place so far as pay was concerned.

These creatures did not hesitate to tamper with the Negro. Induce him to run off to the camps. The owner would frequently follow, and get his negro if he could happen to see him. He was kept out of sight of master as much as possible. This was all generally done by the common soldier, who in all probability, when at home was in the same capacity, a **white slave**.

Capt. O.C. Rounds

Capt. O.C. Rounds figured largely in this batch of Yankee soldiers, acting in the capacity of prv. marshal. Has rendered himself conspicuous, and, at the same time, unpopular among the inhabitants of the neighborhood of Murfreesboro.

It may not be out of place to notice some of his doings. To all appearances is a man of common ordinary capacity, would feel the importance of any high position he might be placed. Take a particular pleasure in making others feel his power, and with all, was deceitful. As instance:

When he first came to this place, imposed on the credulity of some of church going people, by holding out the idea and stating he was a member of the Methodist church. For a time attended meetings regular. What his object could be for this was not known, unless for deeper designs. Was thought by some to be a good religious man.

His operation thus: should any of the picket guard let off his gun by accident or otherwise, it would be reported that they had been shot at by some citizen after night. Next day about a dozen citizens would be arrested, and brought before him. He would order them to be put in confinement for the supposed offence. Some under guard at the court house; others to jail. In several cases a number were sent off to Nashville, and put in the Penitentiary and remain some time, or until they would give a heavy bond and security for their future good conduct.

At one time he and his associate Col. Parkhurst were riding out of town after night, and it so happened, as they were passing, a soldier was in the back yard of Jas. Cothran for the purpose of stealing chickens. Accidently made a noise which startled the dog, and was likely to be caught by it. Fired his pistol in self-defence.

For this alleged offence, supposing they had been shot at by some person while passing along the road, ten persons were arrested and, put in confinement in the court house for a period of time. Many such cases occurred.

And for the greater safety of the Yankees occupying this post, was thought by the powers to disarm all citizens of all guns, pistols, and amunition in their hands, and put the same under the controll of the military authority.

An order is issued to search all citizens house for arms, which is done. On a certain day a regiment is divided into small squads headed with a corporal. Different sections of the town is assigned. They start out simultaneously.

After a fiew hours, they return to head quarters with the articles captured, such as was considered contraband which was an odd mixture of guns. Some that was fine and prized by the owners. These were all diposited in one of the vaults in the court house, with the promise, they should be returned at a proper time. All now under lock and key. It was creditably told that the finer of the guns were packed in a box and shiped off North, as one of the benefits of office.

In making searches at houses the men were disposed to be verry particular in their duty. They were in **drawers, trunks,** and **boxes,** turning every article over, upstairs and down in pantrys, closets, and smoke houses, turning over meat that was packed. In fact, their heads and hands were in every nook and corner. Would be unnecessary to say how many small things not contraband disappeared and was never accounted for to the Provo. Letters did not escape a glance over. One of the family shewed them round in this **honorable** undertaking.

This was a thing the people had never been subjected to before and to their feelings, was verry humiliating.

The capt. becomes acquainted with a business house at the Depot and one of the partners, Mr. Menefee, owned a verry fine horse which he valued highly. The capt. got permission to use him for a short time to ride for his health. He retains the horse, promising he would return it. To wind up the transaction, horse was never returned, but was sold and proceeds never turned over to Menefee. The horse was valued by the owner at three hundred dollars.

The preceeding may be a specimen of northern piety transplanted on a southern soil.

To persue the capt. a little further, one other act will be mentioned and then pass him for a time.

Five soldiers were sent out on their own account, in the neighborhood of Pearces Mill. While there a small squad of Confederate cavalry came on them, and fired, killing one of the party. For this offence about twelve citizens in the neighborhood were arrested brought to town and put in the court house in close confinement under guard. This was for the raid by the soldiers, which the Yankees call bush whackers.

Out of this number of twelve men, it was currently reported about the streets that **two** would be hung for the killing.

The preseumption is the Capt. is sufficintly introduced. To note all the mean acts under his administration would take too much time and paper. Tis quite likely he may be refered to and for the present drop the subject.

June 20, 1862

Among the military characters about here, we have Coln. Lester. Has somewhat the manner of a gentleman, being disposed to be acommodating in his nature, altho he differed with Col. Parkhurst in some things. The citizens (if it could be said, they liked at all), had more for Coln. Lester than any that is on hand. Might be set down as a man a little over common order.

S.D. Baldwin

S.D. Baldwin, one of our esteemed old acquaintances, formally a citizen of this place, was located at Nashville at the time of the breaking out of the rebellion. Was preacher in charge of the McKendree church. He was attact by a **low editor,** by name of **Mercer** who report says was at one time verry active in smugling **quinine** into the rebel lines, making money thereby. By some means the scales droped from eyes. He was converted into a **union man** of the first order.

Also, another deciple by name of Northcott, who was a dear neighbor while at this place, and had received many favors at the hands of B—.

These two characters both being small editors at different points, seek the opportunity of injuring the character and standing of this man by publishing **scurrilous** pieces in their sheets. The former editor calls him "Meroz Baldwin, a little wild swarthy preacher. Speaks of his "Armageddon." Calls him a "violent rebel." "Struts like a Turkey Gobler," and how bad he was. "Scared at the news of the fall of Donaldson." The person attempted to preach on "Cowardice & R." Northcott says, in the "main a clever fellow," then goes on to endorse Mercer. The "out Herods' Herod" or out "devil satan" winds up. "Is one of the vainest men I ever saw." A bunch of **Peacocks** feathers fastened to him would cause him to strut himself to death. **Poor Fellows.** Pity.

Little dogs bark—The mastiff growl!

Such was the present case. These **two dogs,** kept up an incessant baying, which caused the military authorities to take notice of Mr.

Baldwin and suppose him to be a bad man. Was accordingly arrested, imprisoned a while, and ordered to be sent South.

Genl. Buell, understanding what had been done, gave the Gov. to understand that he did not know what he was about. His belief **unlike** the editors. That he was a sensible man and could do the **union cause** more harm than any that could be sent there if he was so disposed. Order was reversed - sent north.

It was all a small affair and brought on by small men. This took place in the Spring.

The Times, June 25, 1862

By June of 1862, things have the appearance of quietness about this portion of the country. The cavalry are keeping up the appearance of watchfulness on their part. Detachments are sent out in all direction every day. They don't appear to accomplish much in the way of capturing "Sesesh."

At one thing they are good. When they return at evening, they have a string of prisoners dangling to the saddle strings which has been captured during the day from the old women.

These were of the non combattants and were known and believed not to be **spies**. None ever went into the camps unless they were pressed. But, for reasons, charges were perfered against them, and they had to go - to wit - Chickens, Turkeys, and Pigs. In all cases, a drum head court marshal is held in every instance. They are executed. Cruel Soldiers!

Distress

Now and then would see some person from the country wearing rather a long face looking about as sorry as the boy who had let his bird loose. What is the matter friend? Why, one of my negros run off to the camps last night, and they wont let me in to look for him. I don't know what to do about it. Have you seen Billy to day? I reckon he could get a pass for me or go with me and get him!

Meet another sorrowful fellow walking round the streets, hands in his pockets, examining all the horses at the hitching posts. Fellow! What are you after? Well! Some of them Yankee pickets came out to my house yesterday and took two of my best horses. I thought I would look round. Might see them and try to get them back. They took them at a mighty bad time for me. I was just about laying my crop by. Some one told me they thought that they saw just such a horse as mine. Can you tell me where I can find Billy? Will get him to go to the camps with me to look for the horse.

Hello, there! I say! Can you tell me where the **Pro. Vos** office is? Some of them devils came to my house yesterday and took two loads corn. This is all they give me. Said I could get my pay by coming to town. I have done so, and I cant get out. They say I must take the oath before I can get a pass to go out. I dont want to do that! Would see them at the devil first.

Another Class

Up steps a young Yankee soldier. Mr! Can you tell me where I can buy some pyes? Direct him to some corner where he can make the purchase. Presently see him on the return with a couple of **"turn overs,"** as he calls them, one in each hand. On one he is making considerable inroad with preceptable satisfaction to himself.

Down the street there you have a picture of three or four Yankees and a cow. Three Yankees are guarding the cow with their bayonets. The fourth one is in the act of "pailing the cow" in his canteen.

About the streets some are playing ball. Others, at marbles. A large number cooking and lugging light bread and **"hard tack."** A portion swinging about, not knowing what disposition to make of themselves.

Now and then some of the more **patriotic** would be sitting in groups around some citizen, venting their spleen on Morgan, calling him by all sorts of names. But an honest man and against the "Sesesh" soldiers generally. Ask the question why they will not stand and make a fair fight, like men, and not be bush whacking so much. Tis a little amuseing to hear the threats of what they would do should they come up or catch Morgan in their rounds. Small Yankee picture.

Grape Vine Telegraph

Meeting citizens generally in groups at some store room, seated on chairs, boxes, and nail kegs, or on pleasant weather some shady place on the streets. At these meetings each man with his knife out and a large splinter of either cedar, or pine wood—whitling. Some one, "Heard any news to day?" "I heard some!' A reliable person told me that a large portion of the Southern army was within twenty miles or less of this place—think it is Starnes cavalry. This is no "grape vine." It is **true**.

I reckon that is so, says another. Saw Mr. S. from Cripple Creek yesterday. He told me he had been out fishing with a dip net and was carrying it along on his shoulder, when four or five of Starnes men came up and asked the way to Mr. S. house. He said they were **thick** all through that part of county.

That looks like some of **Ivys** grape vine. "Grape vine or no grape vine, I believe it," says **Ivy**, and "I should not be surprised they would come in any day."

"Oh! You must be joking." "Well! I tell you what I believe. The boys will be here, and that before long. Mind I tell you," says Font.

Says another, "I have heard that Morgan was in Kentucky playing the verry mischief." They say he has torn up the R. Road, captured ten cars and a little further down captured fifteen wagons, all loaded with army stores.

Now take a stroll across the square to some shady corner. There find another squad all more or less with their knives and splinters busy making long shavings and smoking their pipes. Speaking, "Any grape vine news to day **Ivy**?"

About this time a loitering Yankee comes in, stands about. All is quietness. Nothing but whitling and smoking going on.

Thus the time passes off from one day to another. Each one speculating, when the war will end and their opinions how it will end, and the final results.

Mayor and Aldermen again

Some mention has been made in reference of Mayor and Aldermen. May not be improper to remark that the Mayor and several aldermen resigned, and their places were supplyed by others who submitted to the **imposition** of oath required. This was a proper course under the circumstances. It satisfied the authorities at the time.

As for the oath, in a legal point of view, had no strength. There being different forms for the same object, being constructed by different persons, and likely administered by those who were **not** qualified, and, of course, ment little or nothing.

However it may be a matter of **form** or **war oath**, and those taking receive the form and **not** the substance. But Keep Inviolate.

July 5, 1862
Danger Brewing

We now and then hear of movements across the country of some strange cavalry and their hovering around and through the hills. Reports would say it was Starnes. Others would have it Morgan's, and finally conclude that there were a large force of some sort of "Sesesh" cavalry, which was frequently seen.

But, none of this had been seen by any of the Yankee scouts (possibly, they did not go far enough to get a sight). They, of course, construed it all as a ghost, invented to excite them if possible.

They paid but little attention to any such reports, and, of course, made themselves easy. Still, kept small squads of cavalry galloping out a small distance in the county and back. Should they, while on these scouts come across some wary chicken, it was seen to be captured, taken off a **prisoner** for **life** regardless of old women's protests. Return at evening, all right side up, and as for the thought of danger brewing for them they scouted the idea. The cry of "Wolf" had been sounded too often in their ears. It had no effect on them.

They continued their daly visits to the country. Their forage wagons on the go, bringing loads corn and hay, and the usual addition of poltry and any other article that happened to suit the fancy.

While all this is going on, some mysterious persons are seen strolling about through the neighboring woods, not far from where the pickets generally kept a stand.

They had an excuse, if met by any person, as though they had lost some stock of some kind. May be one would be looking for a sow and pigs and another probably had unfortunately let his cow out and trying to find her. If any of the picket guard come across them, of course their misfortune was made known, were permitted to pass all right and nothing else.

Mention has been made of about a dozen citizens who had been arrested in the neighborhood of Pearces Mill for some bush whacking, supposed to have been done by some of the neighbors. So thought the Yankees. These men were brought in and put in confinement as hostages for the future good conduct of the people there.

It can be seen how things has been progressing in this portion of country for some time past. And every thing in view of the Yankees had the appearance of security. No thought of any **fox** lurking in the neighboring forest, watching an opportunity to gather up the **many soldiers,** who might be out on a solitary foraging expedition to lift poor **Chanticleer** off **his** quiet roost.

It will be recollected that Coln. Forrest had made McMinnville his head quarters for some time past. With his command of Confederate Cavalry had been keeping a vigilant watch over Abraham's **union restorers** at Murfreesboro.

Every thing being now understood as to the position of the Federal army and their position of camps. Forrest determined to make an attact. At once orders the necessary rations to be issued to the soldiers for the march.

On Saturday, July 12, his cavalry forces are put in motion. Takes the road leading from McMinnville to Murfreesboro, traveling slow most of the time, being after night. On his near approach sends out an advance guard, men that was familiar with the locality of the neighborhood.

The Federal picket was usually placed out on the road about three fourth of a mile from the court house. Forrest advance guards. When they are nearly to the place turned off the road, through an old field and got in between them and town. They now go to the road and gallop out to where the picket is posted. (Tis said they were found asleep.) This movement was to lull suspicion on the part of the Yankees.

They are immediately captured without any noise. The way now being clear, a runner is sent to Forrest who now advances with his cavalry in sight of town. His plans, having all been arranged, first to make an attact on the camps at Maneys Spring, next to make an attact on the court house and city hotel where the Federal forces are quartered.

It was now getting early day light. Every thing was quiet. Not a noise to be heard in any quarter. The soldiers quietly **reposing**, possibly **dreaming** of quiet homes, their wives, and children and friends—When—

The Battle of Murfreesboro, and Capture

Sunday morning, July 13, 1862, Coln. Forrest gives the order to advance. They start off at full speed, the horses hoofs making a noise like distant thunder. The men, yelling like wild Indians, **dash** into the camps of the sleeping enemy (this is a short time after day light). The party making the attact at Maneys Spring were a little foiled in their dash. On coming up there was a large cable rope for the purpose of tying horses, stretched some distance across the ground. The cavalry ran against this which took them a fiew minutes to remove it. They fell back, reformed, advanced again, opening a deadly fire on the Federal soldiers through their tents and all that shewed themselves. Fiew of them that had got out of bed.

The firing continued sharp from Forrest forces. In a fiew moments nearly the whole of the tents were in a light glaze. The rebels continued the yell and following up the enemy, which had been thrown into confusion, gave them but little time or opportunity to form a line of battle.

The Federal made several attempts to rally their men and get them in line, but were as often driven from it and could not get the men to stand. They were so panic stricken.

Very little firing was done by them. They at one time attempted to form a breast work with some bailed hay that was on the ground but were driven from this purpose, being pressed by the confederate cavalry. Finally, a large number stampeded, run in all direction by dozens. Some in their shirts and drawers and without hats. Could be seen sculking along the fence rows, cavalry men after them. In one instance a capt. ran off in the country three miles—came in the next day.

Genl. Duffield, who was on the ground in the engagement, was severely wounded and was taken off early in the action.

The fight at this place did not last over three fourths of an hour. The forces surrendered—men, camp equipage, and every thing on the ground to the rebels. The men that were captured was put under guard and sent off immediately and camps all destroyed. This was a complete **surprise** on the part of Yankees.

The sun was just rising, being a calm, clear morning. The citizens were also taken by surprise, doubtful whether a single person was aware that any thing of the kind was suspected or would take place.

During the time, the detachment that had made the attact in town were still skirmishing round the streets and court house, having a bad chance to do much execution as the enemy had the advantage of being protected by the houses and firing from the windows. They had killed several of the rebels in this way. The court house and Hotel was occupied by the Federals.

They had been able to keep the rebels at bay all the morning. After the capture at Maneys Spring the rebels was reinforced, halted in a back street, laid off their havre sacks, blankets, and all other things that would impede their movement.

The attact is now made with renewed energy on the part of the rebels. They dismount, make a rush for the court house. Under a heavy fire reach the doors, but many a brave fellow fell on the way, crossing the street. A pretty strong force enters the court house. The Yankees, being in the upper story, were continuing to fire on any person they could see on the streets.

A surrender was demanded of them. To this they did not shew a willingness to comply. Were then told, if they did not surrender, the court house would be fircd and them in it. Fire at the same time was being started in one of the doors. At this they gave up. The post that was at the hotel held out a little longer after this, but finally, laid down their arms.

The Rebel soldiers in this part of the fight suffered greatly in consequence of having to be exposed all the time from the firing from the windows. The losses was all on their side at this place. It was about 9 ocl. in the day when fighting ceased on the public square.

An order had been given by the Federal officers to fire on all citizens who may be in the streets. This was carried out. One man was killed and one badly wounded from shots fired from a distance. When any person attempted to pass or cross a street would be fired at.

Some time after the surrender on the public square, there were some firing by the sharp shooters who were secreted about corners and in small corn patches. This was without much effect. The shots being at long range, merely had a tendency to put those on their guard who might be out.

*It may be remarked here, the order to fire on the citizens, men, women, and children, is understood to have been a standing order in case of an attact at any time on the place. (Was by Coln. Parkhurst.) This was an unnecessary order, as the Provost Marshal had collected all the guns and ammunition that was to be found. Not lead enough left to make a sinker to a fish line. It was thought there might be some danger still in these "butter nut Sesesh."

While on this subject will introduce to acquaintance one Genl. **Crittenden** from Indianna, who arrived at this place about three days since. His business, it was said, to take charge of some post of command. He must have been a hard case, from a specimen of conversation droped. (Speaking of the southern people) says, "They were not worthy the bread they eat, the cloths they wear, or the air they breathe."

This was quite a hard beginning, for only one or two days acquaintance. But fortunately, his time, proved short with us.

This General put up at a boarding house on the public square. Will speak of him again. A nice gentleman from the north who comes to teach justice and submission to the stars and stripes that has been so wofully abused.

There being one more point to capture, it being more formidable than either the other two. This is one and a half miles from town on the river commanded by Col. Lester and Capt. Hewit of a battery of guns.

It being now about ten oclock in the day, Col. Forrest, after having secured matters in the town, send a detachment over to the Depot where there was a large amount forage. A ware house contained bailed hay, corn, and oats. The Depot building had in it Bacon, flour, and other provisions for army use. These two buildings was fired and three other houses was consumed one—Chas. Watts Hotel.

During the time Capt. Hewit was throwing shells quite briskly to the depot and other parts of the town, striking several houses without any other damage. This was continued for several hours. At times quite brisk, was but fiew that exploded.

Forrest now determined to make the attact on these forces, collects his remaining men. A large number having been detached to guard prisoners.

Strikes out in the direction of the camps. Makes a reconnoisance, draws the men and artillery to the Nashville pike just this side of the pike bridge about a half mile from their camps. At this place they form a line of battle. The camp but slightly protected by a guard.

Forrest sends a small detachment of men in a circuitous rout through the woods. Back of the camp, which was thickly timbered, they pitch in among the tents and set them on fire. In a fiew minutes, they are all burn'd to the ground with all the clothing, papers, and every thing else that is in them. Return without any damage to themselves.

Hewit's battery is shelling the woods briskly in all directions with shell, grape, and canister. Forest, keeping out of the range, and pretty much out of view by the small rises in the ground and the timber, returned to town a time or two and start in another direction. Shelling is still continued, the infantry not having an opportunity to do any thing as the parties had not been near each other. The federals had no information as to the number of men under Forrest. They were working on an uncertainty.

It was now getting near the middle of the day. Forrest now determined to make one more effort to capture the enemy if possible, having been successful so far. Was not disposed to give up. He has a dispatch conveyed to Genl. Duffield, who was severely wounded and at Maneys house, stating that he will capture his forces or lose all his men in the attempt as he has the ability to capture. This was a bold assertion. At the same time commences his march in the direction.

Genl. Duffield sends a dispatch to the command to **surrender** to Coln. Forrest unconditionally. It was about one oclock when Forrest receives a flag of truce and order of surrender.

The Yankees were verry much mortified at this. They were anxious to have a fight, felt satisfied they could hold their ground against Forrest.

A little after one oclock, the news reach town of the surrender. The artillery had ceased firing and arrangements being made to take charge of the prisoners and camp equipage. This closes the fight.

Forrest takes charge of the prisoners, collects all the guns loads them in wagons, also all the camp equipage. Arranges the men for marching orders.

But previous to marching, sends orders to town for the citizens to prepare provisions to be sent out by wagon that would be round for the use of the prisoners. Before marching, the order was complyed with. The necessary quantity was soon procured and on its way to the camps on the river. They were all fed and made as comfortable as the case would permit.

At about 4 ock, every thing being now ready, the order is given to march. They pass through town and by 5:00 in the evening all had disappeared on their way to Mc Minnville to Forrest's head quarters, for the purpose of being parolled.

It was a singular sight to see the number of men that had been captured by Forrest, he being greatly inferior in number not exceeding one **thousand** cavalry. Nearly all armed with a **double barrel shot gun.** The union forces stationed here was fully **Fifteen hundred** men, infantry well armed with a good **Endfield Rifle** and a battery of **four pieces** of cannon.

It was Forrest's superior strategy in this case and having the union men scattered out the way they were found. For, had they been encamped as they should have been for safety, three times the number Forrest had in command, armed as they were with shot guns, could not have effected the capture of the **fifteen hundred infantry** and a good **battery**. May prove a lesson for the future.

Causality of The Battle

The attact at Maneys Spring—there were twenty one union men killed, and two negros that was employed as servants - no confederates. At the attact at the court house, there was twenty three confederates killed and no union men. At the attact on the river there was two on each side killed. The wounded on each side (not having understood the number but suppose it was about equal). There were a good many died afterwards from their wounds.

(A singular coincidence, there being three divisions of union men at one place of attact—all union men killed. Second place—all confederates killed. At the third place an equal—two on each side. The numbers so near the same—total 23 and 25).

There was one citizen, Mr. Nesbit, killed. He was at times a little deranged—could not be persuaided to stay at home at the time of fighting. Mr. Booker was dangerously wounded, having been shot through the body. The confederates fell generally round the public square. Three shot and killed on the north corner. Several between the fence and court house.

Incidents

As a matter of history may not be amiss to note a case or two of **chivalry**. It will be recollected, that mention has been made of Gen. Crittenden who arrived at Murfreesboro so recently from Illinois and the bit of speech he made shortly after his arrival. This specimen takes lodgings with a Mrs. Hagan, who keeps a boarding house on the public square. He was here at the fight (but not fighting).

Forrest's men are making calls round. Sends in card or invitation for the Genl. to make his appearance. He, feeling a little excited, came running down to the room of the ladies with a "dont be alarmed, ladies, I am a married man." Here! presenting his pistols to Mrs. Hagan, his landlady, asking her to surrender him a prisoner of War!!

She in a "gallant" manner, steps to the door, with pistols in hand—Gent. I, in the name of Genl. Crittenden, surrender him a prisoner of war and herewith surrender to you his pistols, treat him kindly as becomes brave men of the South.

The Genl. now steps forward from behind the Lady. Presents himself in a timid, trembling, manner - ordered to step forward. A mule is led up, he mounts and is escorted off in company with a fiew butternuts who leave at a double, quick. This is the last that is heard of the "Secess quillen."

Cap. O. C. Rounds

Cap. O.C. Rounds has had a formal introduction, at another place. He is Pro. Vo. Marshal of this place. He, like many others, was taking a morning nap and was caught napping when calls were made. Then, many waiting at the door, wishing to have a better acquaintance—he having been a considerate man in his way, figured largely for four months in the city of Murfreesboro. Was a well known character.

Well "Sesesh" called on him and wished to have an interview with his honor. They wait some time. No appearance. Take the liberty to walk in and look for him - reported—not **in**. "Sesesh" not satisfied—talk further of "search house." After pulling and hauling things about for a time, Where! do you think they found him? Echo says where! Right in a closet! Half dressed and trembling like a guilty man—he, unlike the Genl. who wished to be surrendered—he wished Mrs. Reeves to hide him under the bed. However, he is hurried out, not being allowed to continue his toilet. A mule is waiting at the door—is ordered to mount.

A hat is given to him. They all start off on their way rejoicing—end of rebellion "crusher."

The confederates took along with them H.S. Pugh, who had been Post Master. He was a very clever man and no harm in him—also, T. Elliott, a half witted young man. Cant see what use there was in that. Unless he was called a union man.

They were both released after going to McMinnville.

At the time the battle came on at this place, there was about a dozen citizens from the country in the court house, confined there for no particular charge. They felt a little uneasy at the time of fighting, for fear some of the Yankees in court house might be disposed to be revenged and do some harm to them. They bar'd their door up—Forrest released them.

July 14, 1862

The next day being Monday, July 14, 1862 a clear, warm day, the citizens from the country came in great number to see what had been going on the day previous. They all find the manner and appearance of **Bunyans Christian**. All had droped that ponderous load from their backs, had floundered through the slough of disposed, were now happy shaking hands and greeting each other - every body appeared to love every body—all eager to gather information about the fight and who was killed and what had been done with the prisoners. Almost every thing else was forgot.

But—There was still a sad thing to perform. The dead was lying unburied. They were all gathered and coffins prepared, and both parties of soldiers were decently buried. No distinction being made as to prefference. Each party buried to its self. They are enemys no longer. Resting quietly. Both have won a soldiers grave.

Hospitals

The next thing that claimed attention was the wounded of both partys. They were attended to with promptness and the best manner the citizens were capable of. All were active in doing something for the wounded.

At the union hospital there were a good many soldiers on the sick list, and had been rather badly provided for by their friends, before the fight, not having had any preparation made for them. Bedding, more than a little straw on the floor and their blankets thrown on that.

The citizens thought they would mend that matter. They set about making bunks and placing the union soldiers in a more comfortable condition. Feeling it a duty that humanity required.

The Ladies administered to the wants of all as best they could. Thought it a duty to be doing something for the wounded soldier. These attentions were bestowed on the **union soldiers**.

The Confederate wounded was distributed among the citizens to wait on in a similar manner.

Return of Soldiers

About the third day after the battle, the Union Soldiers sent to McMinnville to be parrolled began to return. In the evening citizens met them. As fast as they came were received, taken to their houses and entertained in the best manner, were treated kindly. Many made acknowledgement to that fact.

They remained in and about this place about a day and all then disappeared, on their way to Nashville and homes.

Things were moving on pleasantly, the prospects looking bright to all the people from the country. At liberty to pass in and out at pleasure and nothing to molest. The sick and wounded were provided for. Provisions were procured from the country for their comfort.

But how short sighted we are. Did not seem to comprehend what was before us. Our pleasures, at most, was nothing more than exploded visions and hope defered.

July 17, 1862

On July 17, 1862 we are greeted with an advance guard of the union army, making their appearance for the purpose of reoccupying the town. Shortly after, they came with greater force.

This appeared to cast a gloom over the faces of those whose feelings had been buoyed up with a hope that they would have quiet for a time. But, such is the fate of war—they had to submit with a grace that became them.

The Union men took charge of their own men and permitted the citizens to continue the nurseing of the wounded confederate soldiers. As fast as either was sufficiently recovered, they were sent off to their proper destination.

This is about the history of the Forrest raid on Murfreesboro, **now** being occupied by the Federals and matters and things moving as before.

From this on, for some time, nothing of interest transpiring, more than petty annoyances of the soldiers taking the liberty of going in gardens and taking what suited them. This was done in a stelthy way, take fruit off the trees in a half-ripe state, milk the cows in their canteens, steal chickens, and, if caught at any of these tricks, would return impudence, say they were allowed to subsist on the rebels. They were death on an onion patch after night.

Genl. Bragg Moves To Ky

About the first August Genl. Bragg determines to make a move from his position, which is at Pensacola, in the direction of Kentucky. Is supposed his distination is to Louisville for purposes not fully known to the public. He makes a feint, as though he intended taking his course through Murfreesboro, thence Nashville.

The object more likely for this course was to give his trains of wagons time to get into Kentucky with safety and persue his intended object. He has a long trip before him. His rout is North eastern Alabama, through E. Tennessee, through the mountains.

Genl. Bragg, at this time, is making fair headway through the mountains, nothing to interfere with his movements in the direction of Ky. His move is now creating some excitement with the Federals. Arrangements are on foot to arrest his march.

August 20, 1862

Genl. Buell, who on August 20, 1862 is occupying a portion of North Alabama with a strong force of men, now determines to fall back and intercept Genl Bragg in his advance.

About this time, having put his army in A1 condition for moving, orders them to take up the line of march, making his rout from Huntsville through Murfreesboro, Nashville, thence, the pike on from there to Louisville. His whole force falls back, leaving the country he has been occupying, all in the hands of the Confederate.

It proved to be a verry dry time. Water was scarce on the way, dust very deep, the weather quite warm, all this together caused both men and horses to suffer much for the want of water. Notwithstanding all this difficulty, Genl. Buell hurries on his men in the direction of Louisville.

The main body of men was passing Murfreesboro about the last of the month, continued for several days. Retreating men shew a disposition to be destructive. While passing here, several attempts were made to fire the town. A fire was started in the court house on the stairway, and by mere accident was extinguished—another in the Tel. Printing office. This was stoped in time without any injury. Two or three small fires took place, and some doors that was locked up was forced open. The people had to be watchful of their houses at night, not knowing what time a torch might be applyed.

There were many family residences on the road to Nashville that was burned down by the retreating soldiers. A great deal of this firing was done for the purpose of robbery and some for the purpose of gratifying a low, malicious feeling, as they had come more to destroy than to restore the country to peace.

Sept. 5, 1862

Today, about one oclock, the rear guard of cavalry of Buell's army took the line of march in the direction of Nashville, covering the retreat to the great satisfaction of all concerned, being what is called a hard set of men.

But before they had got fairly out of sight of the place—we see a force of Col. Forrest's cavalry, making its appearance on the Lebanon pike, riding in a leisure manner. They were a dusty looking set of men, the cloths all having a dirt colour, their faces pretty much the same appearance. An observer could not well discriminate what their natural colour was, all caused by the great quantity of dust which they traveled through.

However—After they got here and understand the retreating army had not been gone long, they determine to follow, which they did some three or four miles and fire a parting salute at them.

The two armys were left, making their way for the Louisville road. Gen. Bragg struck the road, some distance in advance of Gen Buell. They both occupy the same road in their travel. This continued for some time, Bragg in the lead. Common report says that when Bragg stoped at night, Buell would do the same. Did not take up the line of march the next day until the other did—other report that they were relations by marriages and were known to be together during the march. No doubt, this was slander upon the two Genls. No such transaction took place.

Genl. Bragg turned off the road, shapes his course toward Richmond, Ky. Here he has a battle with a portion of Buell's forces, holds his grounds and after night retreats. The losses was serious to each.

Genl. Buell, now having the road to himself, passes on to Louisville with his men. He remains here some length of time, awaiting an attact from Bragg. The people are very much excited at this place, had great fears that the city would be shelled and cause great destruction of property.

They set to active preparation for defense. Every body with every thing was out fortifying.

The people at Covington, Ky. was also panic stricken. Every fellow with his wheel barrow and pick building up earth works and making ditches for their better protection.

Cincinnatti, last but not least, it began to feel that there was danger. Lawyers, Merchants, and clerks all were summoned to take hold of the pick and spade and bear a part in the protection of the city.

How different are their feelings when trouble is about to invade their hearth stones. Many of those, who are now panic stricken, at other times can sit with a morning paper in hand, leisurely puffing his segar, gloating over the misfortunes and distruction of property of the people in the south. Many who are more loyal at heart for his country than they.

So long as the war keep at a distance from them and theirs are willing it shall go on rather than loose a good fat government contract. Such is human nature.

It is evident that Gen Bragg did not go in Kentucky for the purpose getting into battles. He had another object in view, and if he did fight, it was forced upon him. He wanted provisions and clothing for his army and, as a matter of course, would not refuse to accept of a fiew recruits to his army, if offered.

Gen. Bragg and his army were not idle. They were employed in collecting all the goods they could find suitable for soldiers wear, cattle and horses for army purposes, and did expect additions of men to his army. But his stay was too short to effect much in that part of country.

He fills his mission pretty much to his satisfaction, having collected large quantities jeans, shoes, and other articles suitable for the wants of his men. These are loaded on the wagon trains, turns them in the direction of East Tennessee, ahead of the army, it lying back to give the trains time to get through the mountains in safety. This collection of property was said to be of immense value. The beef cattle and horses were fine.

While this business is going on, Gen. Buell is lying at Louisville with his army fortifying, becomes impatient—starts out in quest of Bragg and his army. He finds them in the act of leaving the country with their booty, undertakes to intercept and cut off the retreat of Bragg, makes forced marches and comes up with him at a small town, called Perryville, Ky.

At this place a hard battle is fought, the losses on each side considered heavy. Bragg held his position, drove back the enemy, attended to the wounded, as well as circumstances would admit, not wishing to hold the place longer. At night he determines to evacuate, leaving a great many of his wounded behind, to fall in the hands of the enemy, not being in a condition to move many on with him.

By this time the wagon trains had been enabled to be far advanced ahead of the army, which was now following on. They pass through the Cumberland Gap without any difficulty—through East Tennessee and on south. The trip was hazzardous, but paid well on his part—but he lost many brave soldiers in carrying out the design.

The part of Kentucky, where the armys have been marching, was very badly watered, the season being so verry dry. It was with great difficulty the soldiers could procure a sufficent supply for their common use.

The place where the battle was fought, there was a small stream. It had, in a manner dryed up, with the exception of holes now and then. Here Bragg had the advantage of the stream for his men. The other army could not procure scarcely any water. They consequently suffered very much from the want of water.

The trip for both armies, particularly at this season of the year, was very trying to man and horses, on account of the deep dust and want of water. The water the soldiers used was from ponds, warm and covered with a green scum, places where stock was in the habit of watering. Some of these ponds - dead animals was found in. But such is the life of soldiers.

Genl. Bragg had escaped entirely out of Kentucky with his army, leaving Genl. Buell in possession of the state, to mend up matters as best suited him.

The public, not being satisfied with Gen Buell on account of his not capturing Bragg as he was known to have the most men in his command. They seek to raise the charge again—that he favored Bragg. They were related and were known to take drinks and suppers together on their marches. These were all false reports. No such thing took place.

However, matters came to the point that Genl. Buell was called on to report himself for an investication of his conduct for not capturing Gen Bragg.

The army he commands is called the army of Ohio. He is now superceeded by Genl. Rosecrans, who takes command. He reorganized the command and it is now called the army of the **Cumberland**.

The first point that Genl. Rosecrans turns his attention is Nashville, Ten. He puts his army in motion, and by the first of Nov. they arrive there, or was expected.

Sept 20, 1862

It is now two weeks since the Yankee army evacuated this place. Everything has the appearance of pease and quietness. The people are beginning to have enjoyment, contrasting the time when we were having so many little annoyances with the impudent Yankee soldiers, who were going in gardens, taking fruit without as much as saying with your leave, sir. But with a reply—it belongs to the government, that the people are all "Sesesh" and their property ought all to be destroyed, and how they started fires in different parts of the town to get the people to run to them so they might rob them. In this they were foiled, as the people suspected the design. Staid at their homes.

But in all this could now and then come across some that had been raised with better principle. At ordinary times would pass for gentlemen. But the majority of the soldiers, and, may be said of officers, were such as are generally found about drinking saloons, gambling shops, dens, in back alleys, in large cities. Most likely, many may have served a term in some state **institution**, from appearances.

Well, we are clear of them, for a time. No Yankees to be seen, nor wished to be, by any one. Begin to feel like they would make us another visit. Thus the time passes until—

November 1st, 1862
Confederate Soldiers Make Their Appearance

By November 1, 1862, the confederate soldiers are making their appearance, in small forces from different points. A regiment or two, said to be from North Carolina, have the appearance of being healthy, stout men.

Also, a portion of Braggs forces from their return trip from Kentucky. Every train from the South brings quite a number in—are setting up their tents round the suburbs of town.

A brisk business is now commenced, collecting army stores—such as Bacon, Flour, wheat, and corn. This is shipped south for safety.

Things was moving on in a quiet and easy manner, considering the war times. No one is molested in doing business of any sort.

The soldiers, when they made purchase of any article, were disposed to pay and were liberal in doing so. They had quite a variety of money amongst them. Verry little of it was of much value but appeared to answer the purpose with them. Some of the money had not much better look than a picture out of a newspaper, and then all kind of promises to pay some way.

The soldiers were very deficient in camp equipage, did not have half the articles that was actually necessary for their comfort and convenience. Yet they appeared cheerful under these difficulties. Scarcely ever would be heard a complaint. Any thing would satisfy them.

Their clothing was warm and substantial, but not much uniformity in appearance—some gray, butternut, or brown, and others of rather a dirt colour, which on parade gave a raged look as to uniform. Hats and caps of various forms, colours and shapes, got up substantial, but not fine.

Under this homely garb, there were something which is peculiar to the people south, an easy manner, a warm friendship, social feeling, strong attachments for friends, and the ingredience that constitute the southern gentleman.

The confederate army still on the increase at this place. Army stores (provisions) now coming in from the country in large quantities. Shipping off South—none retained here, more than for present use of the soldiers.

By this time quite a force of cavalry had been collected. They are now out skirmishing in neighborhood of Nashville. At times are quite venturesome, will run the Yankee pickets almost within the limits of Nashville. In this way, the pickets are kept annoyed.

The Federals are actively engaged, fortifying the streets of Nashville. The principle streets leading into Nashville have ditches cut across, cotton bales and sand bags piled up for breastworks to keep the rebel cavalry off.

Communication was, in a manner, cut off from Nashville, but fiew were allowed to pass the lines. There were some that would run the blockade, as it is called, with a fiew goods to sell. Goods were selling high south of the Federal lines. Thus, matters wore on, without much interest or any thing that was exciting.

December 15, 1862

By December 15, 1862, Gen. Bragg had received about the extent of his forces, they having been arriving for some time in small detachments to this place. During the time active arrangements were on foot, collecting all the provisions that was to be had for the use of the army and continuing to ship south.

Skirmishing with cavalry continued frequent in the neighborhood of Nashville, and at times, would be daring—running the Federal picket guard into the city limits. This was repeated frequently.

Forrest and Morgan made a slight attact at two places on Nashville, more for the purpose of drawing off attention and taking an opportunity to burn some bridges and destroy the R Road.

The armies, in other quarters to all appearance, were quiet at this time, possibly with an eye to the doings in this part of the country. From every indication, it was thought a battle would evidently take place between Genl. Bragg and Genl. Rosecrans who is now in command of the federal forces at Nashville, called the army of the Cumberland. This battle, should it take place, was thought would be about **Stewarts Creek**, which is about eight miles from Murfreesboro. The Federal cavalry would venture out in large bodies up the pike, skirmishing almost every day. They having got themselves fortified in a temporary manner in and about Nashville. Nothing in these ventures would seriously happen.

Genl. Bragg had now nearly completed his collection of army provision. His whole forces, being quartered at this place, determine to send Gen Smith south and in a short time follow. Accordingly as **was his** intention, he posted Gen. Smith off with Ten Thousand men in the direction of Mobile.

After remaining at Murfreesboro for some time after Gen. Smith departure, things had taken a change. He was threatened with an attact by Gen. Rosecrans. It was **not** Gen. Braggs wish or intention to risque a battle at this place, but to fall back to a more eligable point. In this, he is overruled.

A meeting of the officers was had and it was unanimously agreed they would meet the enemy at this place, throwing Gen. Bragg in the minority.

December 25, 1862

Gen. Jno Morgan was, on Dec. 25, 1862, on an expedition in Kentucky with his cavalry. His return is now looked for. Gen. Wheeler, with his cavalry forces are rangeing through Williamson, Davidson, and Rutherford counties, harrassing the enemy at every opportunity and doing good service in his way.

He, now, commences heavy skirmishing with the enemy cavalry in the neighborhood of Triune, driving it in the direction of Murfreesboro. The rains had fallen at this time, quite heavy, which made the roads difficult to travel when off the pikes, being through a rocky and cedar portion of the country.

Gen. Rosecrans, who is now at Nashville, on 25th gives orders to prepare for an advance move in the direction of Murfreesboro. Accordingly every thing ready, the necessary rations issued, tents and camp equipage packed up, they now take up the line of March on the pike leading to Murfreesboro, making short marches, having their skirmishers out in different directions.

About the same time, Gen. Bragg and staff commences the selection of a battle ground, which occupies them a day or two to get the proper position. It is finally accomplished.

The Battle ground lies, the nearest part, about two miles from Murfreesboro on the road leading to Nashville, running rather an East & West course. The centre of line, about the crossing of the R. Road and pike, and extends in length about two and a half miles, running across the lands of Esqr Cowan and near his dwelling. Cowan had to leave his premises in consequence of being on the battle field. There being a good many out houses on the premises and was thought might interfere in getting a fair vision, Genl. Bragg ordered the out houses to be burned out of the way, reserving the family house, it being a large, two story brick. Unfortunately the wind was the wrong way. While burning the others, it took fire and had the same fate.

This all appeared hard, but could not well be avoided. This happens two or three days before the battle takes place. The battle ground lies generally level and is said, by those who are experienced in such matters, to be well suited for the purpose.

The Scene Begins To Thicken

Every thing now being ready, Gen. Bragg commences to form his lines of battle. Every thing is in motion, the men anxious for the fight, and all felt certain of a victory. By the 30th of December, Genl. Bragg, having his men placed in position of line of battle, now waiting the approach of the enemy. All apparently anxious to get an early sight, as though they were watching for common game.

Gen. Wheeler is not idle. He is skirmishing and gradually drawing on the enemy to battle. They are approaching cautiously, and in heavy force. It was the intention of Gen. Rosecrans, in making his advance on Murfreesboro, to throw out heavy flanks, bringing the centre on the Nashville pike, his right flank about the Salem pike and by that means surround Bragg and his army. For some cause, this part of the program of march was not carried out.

He continues to advance his army slow and with caution, his cavalry skirmishing ahead. Most of the time, there had been great quantities of rain fallen. The ground, being saturated, proved difficult to get artillery along through the woods. It being broken, rocky, and thickly set with cedar timber through which they had to pass before they could reach the battle ground.

They finally reach—commence forming the lines, column after column, advance, and take their place until all complete. The lines are formed, the day is past, nothing is heard but now and then a fiew discharges of artillery by the skirmishers which finally dies out. Night comes on. Soldiers, lying on their arms to rest—to dream of homes, of wives and little ones—per chance, that may be fatherless ere another day.

Genl. Bragg commenced forming his line of battle on Sunday and by Tuesday had completed his arrangements, being now ready to receive his expected **guest**. All was quiet.

Genl. Rosecrans has arrived and taken up quarters for the night. Having put matters in order, visited for the evening with the necessary caution in case of a disturbance during repose. During the evening there had been heavy cannonading between the parties, as an introduction—no damage done, more than to waste a little amunition on the occaision and to shew off a little war thunder.

The two are now in a line of battle fronting each other. Gen. Bragg, understanding the position of the enemy, wishing to avail himself of a little strategy, sets a **trap**. On Tuesday evening about dusk he detaches a division of men from his right wing, sends them to his extreme left. Being under cover of darkness, they cautiously get a convenient position to the enemy near as possible, lie down on their arms, remain so during the night without fire or any thing to attract attention.

The two armys as they lie on the ground are estimated—that of Bragg, from reliable information (one of the officers) who knew the strength, stated in round numbers there were **Thirty two Thousand** men.—Rosecrans, from the best information, was variously estimated from **Forty Five Thousand** to **Sixty Five Thousand** men.

The Battle

Wednesday, December 31st, 1862. Being a clear, bright morning, the sun rising without a cloud to obscure, a frost the over night, mild weather to the feelings. It would seem that all nature was rejoiceing after having been shrouded for so many days with clouds and storms. But, it is about to witness one of Joshuas battles (modern), with the roar of cannon, the clash of arms, the dying, and the dead.

Genl. Bragg, it will be perceived, had massed his men on his extreme left wing at early dawn, commenced a heavy assault on the enemy by his artillery that was stationed there and a charge of infantry, taking by supprise. The cannonading, at first, was at intervals. In a very short time became furious. The musketry, peal after peal, charge after charge, kept up incessantly after the retreating enemy - and by eight oclock, had driven the right wing of Rosecrans near to the Nashville pike, throwing it in the form of an L.

This move took the Federals by supprise. They were not looking for a battle to come off at so early an hour. Some had not dressed themselves, others were in the act of adjusting their clothing. Some had taken the artillery horses to water, could not get back in time to hitch up. They were completely demoralized; however, made the best show of fight that could be done, under circumstances.

This is the **Trap** that is set the evening before. The **String** is pulled and to the dismay of the **blue birds**, some Twenty five hundred find themselves entraped as prisoners. They, like men, submit to their fate and are marched off the field, and, in addition, some twenty pieces of cannon, among the number some highly finished. The killed and wounded in this branch of the battle was not serious to either party.

Genl. Rosecrans, by nine oclock, had rallied his men, and came up to the fight. Cannonading became quite heavy on both sides which was kept up incessantly from Braggs and Rosecrans left and right wing to the centre or the crossing of R. Road and pike. The small arms now opens with tremendeous vollies on each other. They now become more determined. It was charge! And recharge! Alternately drive and be driven in turn. The Federal had fallen back in a thick wood, being persuid by the Confederate poring on them a deadly fire. They now return a galling fire on the Confederates which more exposed being in the open field, nothing daunted, make heavy charges on the artillery batteries and by dogged determinedness wrest from the enemy.

As fast as the lines would be broken by loss, they would close up and push forward as though life was of little value to them.

Thus the battle raged nearly the whole day, the musketry keeping up a continued rattle along the lines, cannon booming, sending their deadly messengers in each others ranks, balls flying, shells bursting in every direction, tearing every thing before them in the course. Limbs falling and bullets whizzing through the air like hair. The men became furious. As fast as the front line thined, they would close and rush forward.

Both officers and men, equally determined to do their duty, would rush forward to battle lines, warring first the one then the other in the deadly strife.

Toward evening, the firing slackened off. The musketry had entirely ceased. The cannon would at intervals discharge and finally withdraw for the day, it now being late in the evening. Many brave and gallant fellows fell to day, numbered with the dead.

The confederates, holding the battle field at the close. This, the first days of fight, had the wounded of both sides gathered up and disposed of in field hospitals as well as the case would admit of—the Federals having fallen back about two miles from the battle ground.

The killed and wounded said to be decidedly the heaviest on the part of the Federal. They fought bravely after they got fairly at it. But, not so determined by half as the Confederate soldier. They were fighting for their homes and fire sides. They were on their own soil and defending it.

Instance—A young man, **F. James**, was killed in less than a quarter of a mile of his mother's house in battle while on duty, gallantly defending his soil and fireside.

And another—Col. J.B. Palmer, who was stationed on the right wing of the army in sight of his own house during the battle, was **wounded** in the defence of his home.

Such things as these will make men fight, no matter whether they may be in the right or wrong cause—home is sacred.

2nd Days Battle—Thursday Jany 1, 1863

On the second day of the battle, Jan. 1, 1863 the morning opened clear, bright sunshine, cold, having a heavy frost and slight freeze on the ground. All was quiet, but little firing is heard, more than a boom from a cannon now and then as a kind of feeler for the enemy.

As the Federal had fallen back two miles, the Confederate was having the dead of both sides gathered up and buried. This is on Gen. Bragg's left where the battle was the hotest. From the centre to his right there had not been much engagement.

The confederate lines of battle extended through Cowans field, commencing at the river, passing a pond on the road and R. Road. Just back of the lines the men were busied in throwing up temporary earth works by piling the fence rails and throwing dirt on them and waiting the approach of the enemy.

The day was passing off without much appearance of a battle. The Confederate soldiers, standing in a line of battle in expectation of the approach of the enemy every moment.

The Federal were making an advance, but it was done in a cautious manner—at intervals would throw a shell or shot, feeling the way.

At the same time were not idle on the left wing—they were busy throwing up temporary works. By evening had fortified themselves, were in a good condition to receive an attact or repel one.

Later in the evening, having concentrated their forces on their left wing, commence an engagement, and in a short time a general engagement which lasted until about dark. The battle raged furiously for the time, both with artillery and small arms, neither willing to give the other the advantage of ground. At night are found occupying the same ground they commenced on. The firing, having ceased for the day, the wounded was attended to, as usual. The losses of killed and wounded on both sides was heavy—all quiet during night.

This part of the battle was on Gen. Bragg's right wing and Gen. Rosecrans left—had not participated but little in the first day fight.

Some time after night a rain came on and lasted until morning, which was cold and chilly - the ground being saturated with water.

Genl. Wheeler

At this time, Genl. Wheeler was busy, engaged with his cavalry force at Lavergne on the pike to Nashville, dealing heavy blows on the escort of the wagon trains of Gen. Rosecrans army—capturing a large number of wagons, horses, and army stores—destroying them by burning what he could not move off. He had a hard skirmish fight, which did not last long - took some prisoners - the losses, but slight on either side of killed and wounded.

But the loss to Gen. Rosecrans army was an item of some importance. They, having been ordered front with five days rations in their haver sacks, which had now become almost exhausted. Some of the R. Road bridges to Nashville had been destroyed. No other chance for provision, but to transport by wagon. The prospect was anything but encouraging to hungry soldiers, who felt quite exhausted from cold, hunger, and fatigue.

It began to look like death staring them in front, and hunger in the rear. This could not now be helped. There were more work still to be done before the difficulty could be overcome.

There were a quantity of amunition with the wagon trains for the Federal army, which Gen. Wheeler destroyed. He proved to be quite a **thorn** in the **side** of the Federal army.

3rd Day Fryday, Jany 2nd, 1863

On the third day of the battle, Jan. 2, 1863, both armys were watching the others movements very closely. Rain continued near all day. The ground and the roads became quite muddy, in places almost impossible for wagons or artillery. The day had the appearance of passing off without a battle until late in the evening. Cannonadeing began to be heard at intervals along the lines from each side, continued to increase in quick succession. In a short time the excitement was great—the cannon, roar after roar, along the lines - the musketry, rattle at intervals - evidence the contest was strong and determined.

Officers, moving in quick succession, encouraging their men. Men fighting furiously, like life was of little value—charge after charge on each others lines, dealing death at every blow, lines wavering at each succeeding charge. This continued until about dark, when the firing ceased, and each drew off holding near the same position they occupied.

In a small poppaw thicket, near the river, the dead and wounded lay thick. The contest was short, but was fought with spirit by both parties.

This is on Gen. Bragg's right wing. The engagement was brought on by Genl. Brackenridges corps, which fought under disadvantage. The losses to each was heavy. But the Confederate suffered the most in killed and wounded, being more exposed. This, for the time, was the hardest fought.

The Federal, having advantage by earth works, which they hastily threw up, and clifts of rocks which they could scene themselves from the fire of the Confederate—and then they had massed their men, at least three to one. The wounded were all collected and brought in to town to the hospitals. It had been raining slightly nearly the whole day and continued after night.

4th Day, Saturday, Jany 3rd, 1863

On the fourth day of the battle, January 3, 1863, in the fore part of the day, there was not much indication of a general engagement. Now and then a discharge from a cannon could be heard, as feeling for the enemy. This was continued at intervals during the day. Slight rains came on which added to the disagreableness of the soldiers situation.

But, just about dark a heavy cannonading was commenced on both sides. Musketry rattled furiously for about a half hour and finally died out. This was short but a very severe engagement. The killed and wounded was heavy on both sides.

The soldiers, being now nearly woarn out with fatigue and exposure and no recruits to offer relief, they now begin to flag in exertions.

Genl. Bragg now determines to make a retreat, and so the order is made to that effect. The order had been contemplated early in the day but had not been generally known among the men and was not known by the citizens until about night. Although a great many soldiers had the appearance of moving off early in the evening by their coming to town in twos and threes at a time.

Genl. Bragg's Retreat From Murfreesboro

Soon after the battle on Saturday evening, Gen. Bragg commenced his retreat from this place, all his army stores having been sent off by R. Road during the week with the exception of enough for present purposes. His wagons, loaded with all his camp equipage and out on the road, ready for orders. In fact, nothing was left that was of much value for his purpose. His men all fell back, in good order - every thing was in motion. The retreat was quiet and undisturbed.

By eleven oclock at night, the army had all passed through town from the battle field. The wounded had been gathered up, as was usual. Many that had but slight wounds were sent forward by the cars and other ways. Those that were badly wounded, of course, were left in the hands of surgeons. By morning, every thing had the appearance of quietness, it being Sunday, but fiew to be seen in the streets.

Genl. Rosecrans army was in the act of making a similar move at the same time that Gen. Bragg was. Many of his regiments had returned as far back as Nashville, and it was with difficulty he could get his men rallied. They, too, like that of Bragg's men were tired, hungry, and worn out with fatigue. Did not shew much further interest, how the result would terminate. But, by threats, they were induced to remain longer.

By this time, he gets information that Gen. Bragg was on the retreat, and of course the field was open to him to take possession, which he did in due time.

If Bragg had held his position **six hours** longer, the field would have been his without a doubt.

The reason of Braggs falling back, at the time he did was he had no reinforcement and but little expectation of getting any, and it was currently reported about this time that Rosecrans was about receiving a heavy reinforcement from Kentucky. He, of course, knew his ability. Was satisfied he could not stand against a new levy of fresh men with his already worn out army, and, in fact, had weakened his force too much in the start by sending off south the men he did. Bragg had insufficient forces to meet such numbers as Rosecrans had in his command at the battle of **Stones River**.

He and his men did gallant fighting against a **foe** whose force was near two to one of his. In justice to him and his men it may be said that they made a masterly retreat. But by so doing, it made Rosecrans the **Hero** of Stones River Battle by six hours or there about. This may appear to be a nice point of calculation.

Draw Battle

Now, it is evident, from what can be gathered on both sides of the case that it may be settled. The Battle was a **drawn** one, neither having much right to claim a victory. It appears that both armys were about, or was performing the same move about the same time.

But the move of Bragg was a proper one, for could he have held the field in the place of Rosecrans it would have proved of little value to his army as a position to hold against an invading army. Murfreesboro is so located that it can be approached in every direction, aided by good turn pikes. The building of fortification would be mere waste of time, as they would likely be flanked by approach from any direction.

And then, the country had been foraged over as much as it could conveniently bear, and Bragg could gain but little by remaining there. The proper base of supply (Nashville) being in the possession of the Federals.

It having rained, more or less, during the night of the retreat caused the roads to be quite muddy and heavy for wagonage and soldier traveling. It was not a cold rain, as might be expected at this season of the year; consequently was not so disagreeable as might be anticipated.

January 4, 1863

January 4, 1863 being Sunday was clear and pleasant. There were still a small force confederate cavalry remaining behind to watch the movements of Rosecrans army. His army engaged, pretty much all day, feeling round the neighborhood. Every now and then would throw a shell. Besides this every thing had the appearance of quietness. Very little passing about the streets.

The surgeons were quite busy dressing the wounds of soldiers brought in from the battle field. Their operations resembled a butchers stall—here and there a soldier laid upon a table, under the influence of cloriform, undergoing amputation of arms and legs, which were thrown in a corner of the room—and, from the manner that many of them worked at the business, it would seem that they would be better employed working on the leg of a **calf**, than a man, scarcely distinguishing a tendon from an artery.

Unfortunate for the poor soldier who has to be the subject for these **quacks** who are sent to the army or go to learn their business. This humanity?

The three college buildings were used as hospitals, all the churches, several of the store rooms, and several large dwelling houses. The seats out of the churches and shelving and counters out of the store rooms. Nearly all the families had one or two wounded men in care.

Entrance of Rosecrans

Monday, Jany 5th — Being a clear day, about nine in the morning. The Federal cavalry make their appearance in the streets of Murfreesboro with guns in hands and thumb on the cocks, looking round in a suspicious manner, ready to repel any attact that might be made on them. After riding round the square of the court house, seeing no danger they leave.

In a short time after, the infantry enter with a brass band at the head of the column, playing martial music, blowing and beating their instruments, as it were their intent to burst them. The drums kept up an incessant clatter and the shrill fifes a mingled squeak. The soldiers, Tramp! Tramp! Tramp! The heavy artillery lumbering over the paved streets. The loaded baggage wagons keeping up the chorus of the trains. It was like bedlam let loose to terify and drive the devils dam'd.

And there is Genl. Rosecrans and staff, with banners floating, prancing horses champing their bits, the riders supporting drawn swords as the emblem of authority. Bonapart, in his grand entres' in Paris, did not enjoy greater satisfaction on the occaision than did our **hero** of Stones River on his entrance in Murfreesboro. With a flourish of the sword as becomes a conqueror and at the signal word, Halt!! the moving columns are motionless—"I have seen! I have conquered!"

They now break off in detachments, commence the selection of locations for camping. Every thing now begin to be in a stir. Their provision having run short - soldiers, hungry and tired out - they make the best shift for the time. Now, begins death and destruction to the four footed beasts, all the cattle, hogs, sheep, and poltry, or any thing that came in the way - even the **milk cows** of citizens met a common fate. It mattered not whether it was union or "Sesesh" property they were using, hunger has no bounds.

While this was going on a hurried preparation was also on hand. There were large numbers of wounded lying on the field to collect. Ambulances are busy running for the wounded. They commence fitting hospitals in a better manner for accommodation of the wounded. The confederate army opened a number of hospitals. They had no bunks. The best they could do was to procure clean straw, lay some on the floor, spread a blanket, lay the patient down and cover with other blankets. In this way they lay in rows over the floors. Had been filling the hospitals with both classes of soldiers, up to the time of the retreat.

Their stock of medicines was on a limited scale, and, of course, could not do the justice to the soldier that necessity required. Confederate surgeons were left behind with their wounded men.

Remark Of Battle

Genl. Rosecrans, in forming his line of Battle at Stones River, had an eye to flank Gen. Bragg. His plan was to place a heavy force on his right wing under command of Gen. McCook and hold the attention of the confederates, if possible, in that direction. While he would with his left wing swing round to the Lebanon pike and march into Murfreesboro. By this means double on Gen. Bragg. His forces was fully sufficent to do it.

When the question was asked of McCook, if he could hold the enemy at bay until the manouver should be performed, his reply, "I can hold the place against any force that Bragg may send here."

(The result of the matter has been refered to in a previous note, of Bragg having sent forces against the command of Crittenden and caught them napping.)

But had McCook been able to have carried the intended order out, the result would, in all probability, been different. Bragg, by sending the forces he did the evening before from his right to the left, weakened his strength materially so much that had the order to McCook been sustained, Gen. Rosecrans would have had but a small duty to perform, to have made the flank movement and brought the left wing of his army into Murfreesboro.

Situation

This is contended by military men to be one of the best strategetic points in the state. The country round, generally level, and good pikes from every direction, centreing to this point - should a foe be disposed to pass from South, say to Kentucky - he can be cut off either on the east or west and at the same time hold an army at Nashville at bay.

But Nashville, as a base for army stores and fortifications in that way, has its prefference. Military men are as often in error of judgement of the correctness of things as those who have no pretention.

Of Generals

In comparison of Genls. Rosecrans and Bragg, there is but little difference in point of intellect. Both might come under the head of second class Generals. Rosecrans is overrated in point of capacity, but his men are taught to believe that he is invincible - and when he makes a move that thing is bound to take place. Possibly this may be a part of their tactics. Be this as it may, he appears to have the confidence of his men.

As a man, he makes a fine appearance on horse back, or in a picture, as the case may be.

Genl. Bragg, he, unlike the other is generally underrated, does not at all times get the credit he is entitled to. Is sometimes charged by some for the want of tact in the management of his affairs. This may be by those who know the least of what his designs are. He has one trait - he can make a hard fight, and if pushed close can get out of the way and not be caught. His men respect him but are not disposed to worship. He does not make a fine appearance on horseback nor on paper. But has long since learned to make a **Mark**.

While on this head, it may not be out of order to speak of others, that is now in the armys and have been.

Genl. Lee, of Virginia, may be placed at the head of the list of Genls in all the states. He is serving in the capacity of Confederate Gen. During his service there has been pitted against him some five or six Union Gens. They have all made their "gallant dash" at him, and retire, for some cause, not public—but, he still stands unflinching.

Genl. Boureguard, of S. Carolina, acting in the capacity of Confed. Gen. He may come next on the list - is a first class engineer of fortifications and army movements. Has not done so much fighting as Lee, but appears to have tact in watching his points. Checks when his time comes to play.

The unfortunate Gen. Sidney Johnson of the Confed. army, killed at Pittsburg Landing. He may be placed among the first as a commander. His time was short. Had his plans been carried out at that battle, results would have been quite different. He went there under wounded feelings, determined to sustain himself or die in the attempt.

Genl. McClelland (Union), may be classed best of that side of the question, but not a first class Gen. He is a high minded man of good principle, much better than any that has succeeded him as a Genl.

Gen. Buell may come in with McClelland. He, like the other, had not much opportunity to shew what he might do upon a pinch. He, too, was superceeded. He entered into the war as a rebellion, under different principles to what it is now assuming.

The balance of Union Genls., say in Virginia army, reminds of Cock fighting - country fellow comes along with his dung hill cock under his arm - proposes to bet his chicken can whip - is taken up. He gaffs his cock, drops him in the pit - makes a pass or two. Sock, goes the opponents gaff through its head. There!—dead cock, in the pits—Investigate—report.

Such quick changes in succession is going on among the Genls. that all appear to be dead cocks in the pit. Scarcely give one general a chance to try his metal before he is called on to report at some point for investigation.

Soldiers

As a fiew of the Genls. have been introduced, it may not be improper to give the soldier an introduction. We shall likely have to travel on together for some time—and time will shew whose acquaintance we have made. It is not the expectation, or intention, to draw a correct likeness of them, or of their sayings and doings, but it may be such that you may know them on first acquaintance.

The Yankee soldiers, as we see them, take them as a body of men in appearance. They are fine looking, have regular uniforms, all sky or deep blue. They are all taught to drill (probably not to be surpassed); wear either slouch hats, or scull caps with badges, some with a black feather, others without; name of place they are from and number of regiment; some with shoes; some with boots, moderate length, others with boots appearantly nearly to the ankle.

Language from nearly all nations—Irish—Spanish—Italian—Canadian—English—Dutch—a fiew Americans—and last, but not least, a large list of the decendance of Ham—by some, called contrabands—by others, men of colour.

It would be injustice not to say they were all true and Loyal men to the country in which they were born.

As, says one, I am fiding for te ol stars and strips dat my faders fot for.

Meet another—Hay, be jabers! have ye got inna whisky ye can let a fella have a we dhrop? Come now, trate a man who is fiten for the blessed auld Stars and Strips of our countlevy.

Ellow there! Can I put up my -ose in that -ouse and get a glass of -hale? I'm a hunion soldier.

Another class - de white foks - da have all plade out now—I've jined de rigment - am gwin to fite de Sesesh!

Now and then may hear a native praising the old stars and stripes and muttering something about preserving the union, freedom and crushing out the rebellion.

Pass on, taking items out of the mass, found some that is impudent, some brazen, some insulting, some that had the appearance of having a mother; some gentlemen among them, and others that had grown up by chance and merely vigetated, not knowing how or why.

They are great feeders—see them passing with their arms full bread, bags of potatos, apples, or poltry. Are great on pyes or half moons, as they call them; though, at first, were a little cautious about eating for fear they were "pisoned." They finally got in the way of eating a famous pye called the "gutta percha"—said to have been invented and got up by one of the citizens on corner East Side of the public square. Recipie as given, for making dough—water and wheat flour, worked until tough - roll out in round cakes - dryed apples - a little nut - place these on half of the surface of cake - turn the other over. This is what is called half moon - bake to liking - warranted only to digest in a Yankees stomach. These found ready sale. An onion patch would not admit more than two visits to clean it out. Milk cow in canteen - drink it immediately. The under officers looked stiff in their uniforms, as though they were not used to fine clothing. They were disposed to put on airs and speak short to their men, who, perhaps, were their superiors at home.

Still there was a class men who belonged to the army called Chaplins, Christian Commissioners, for the ameloration of soldiers morals? Preach about, and when a chance offers no compunction of conscience (may the devil get his share of such men). "Gobble up," as they call it, small articles of value. Books and articles of furniture. These they send home, as trophies.

To wind up this side of the picture, will conclude in the language of a Yankee officer: One Col. ask the question of another - Col., what kind of men have you, in your command? Well, Sir, if you will go to any city, visit drinking saloons, corners of streets, sleeping on cellar doors and back allys, you will have an idea of the class of men I have with me—the d-dest lot out of h-l.

The Other Side Of The Picture

The Confederate soldiers, commonally called gray backs, "Sesesh" and rebels. In appearance of uniforms, at first sight are not very inviting, at least not so military looking as one might expect. Some have gray suits, some all brown, or "butter nuts," some gray and brown, and some made of rather a dirt colour. Some wore hats of different shapes and styles, some blue caps, other gray, or dirt colour. Some with boots; large numbers with shoes.

When on drill, they go through the motion quite well to a close observer. But at a glance, does not appear so well - in consequence of such a variety of colour of clothing, which gives them rather a ragged look.

Unlike the others just described. In Language, they appear all to speak the same tongue. They have a fiew Negros (as they call them), as servants along with them, who have the appearance of being quite "loyal to their masters." They shew no disposition to leave them. As for eating, as a general thing - they appear to have verry little care about it - take anything that is convenient - go on without complaint.

Their mode of preparing their provision is some what different from that of the Yankee. As for light bread, they care little or nothing about it. Call it d-d gun wadding. They have their flour and meal dealt out to them. They to suit their own notion. They make what they call biscuit - rather a hard article though. Make corn bread, which they are most generally fond of. Don't object to delicacies, when they can get. A great number like whiskey, will run great risques to obtain it. If they go into a garden or orchard, it was with your leave sir. Were disposed to pay for every thing they get - and were liberal about it - although, some would slip a chicken slyly off its roost, and not think much harm in doing the trick.

In their ranks you find almost all professions and business. Lawyers, Doctors, Merchants, Farmers, students of college, and **Preachers,** unfortunately, and the best of mechanics of all kinds.

When among these soldiers, there was on every day, ease about their manner. True, they did not have so much of that formality that we see in the manner of the Yankee soldier.

Officers and men, when off duty, were appearantly upon an equality. In a common way, would approach in a familiar manner each other - and why not? The men in ranks were worth as much in a pecuniary point as the officers - stood as high in society - and why not in the army?

Take them with all their rough appearance (with fiew exceptions), they generally appeared disposed to conduct themselves in a gentlemanly manner.

The under officers did not have much of the saloon swagger about them, (though some might have been familiar at such place). They were disposed to treat their men in as pleasant manner as they knew how, no use to put on airs.

The Confederate cavalry, as horsemen, were superior to the Federal. They had the nack of sitting on a horse more at ease. When the horse was in a trot or gallop, as the case might be, did not bounce up and down as a majority of the Yankee riders do. They save their horses, unless compelled to move fast. They ride slow, walk, or trot. The Yankee, he, soon as mounted starts off in a fast gallop. The Confederate carry but little baggage with them on horse back. The other, besides the man, is a pack horse.

The best cavalry riders that was seen were those from Texas. They had practiced so (many of them), could lay down a half dollar, start his horse at full speed, swing off, hang by one leg and pick it up, and adjust himself again, throw a larriett over the head of a pig or anything else while in a gallop.

Have now fairly introduced the two classes of officers and men to the reader. Have endeavored to do so without partiality to either party. Having just disposed of one, will now take up with the other (new series) and travel on, and picture as we go.

January 6, 1863

We now return. As we left a preparation going on for the purpose of getting the wounded in a better condition. The hospitals were all being fitted with the soldiers of both armys. Surgeons still very busy, amputating arms and legs and bandaging shot wounds of soldiers.

A great number of families had taken one and two of the confederate soldiers to nurse. It was now getting quite cold. Wood was scarce and hard to procure. Garden fences now came in requisition, more pulled down for fuel. The confederate soldiers fared badly, at first. There was great suffering among them. Their physicians did all they could under the circumstance. The Federal soldiers were cared for before the other could be looked after. At first great numbers of the Confederate died—in fact, so fast that coffins could not be procured for them.

A long ditch would have to be made, soldiers roped up in their blankets. In this way, laid in close to each other and covered up.

There was about one hundred buried in the garden of the Soule Female College. This building was used for the confederate hospital, was called No. 1 Confederate. They did several every day at each hospital for some time. The whole town appeared to be one general hospital.

Articles of provisions of every sort about this time was getting scarce and difficult to procure at any price. Citizens could scarcely obtain any thing in the way of eatibles.

A system of foraging now commenced. Large trains of wagons with guards were sent out every day and hauled in from the Farmers their corn, fodder, and hay, and many times scarcely leaving any thing behind for the familys to subsist on. Take their bacon and, generally, all the poltry. Some times they would pretend to give a receipt for not more than one third—contended they were authorized to subsist on the rebels. Go to a farm yard, deliberately knock off the fence plank, load up, and bring it to town—though a large portion of this kind of lumber was used for making bunks for the wounded soldiers.

Cedar fences began to disappear at a rapid rate. Wagons on the go all the time, hauling rails to town, but little use to make any complaint. Had to stand and look at the destruction of property that was going on. The weather was more mild than otherwise for the season.

It did appear that the federal army had come with redoubled determination to destroy every thing before them. They shewed more ill nature in every thing they did than the year before. More disposed to tack on everybody as Sesesh whether they were so or not. This may have been an excuse to do the depradation they did. Not half the liberty was allowed to the people that was previously. They were not so social, did not take the liberty of walking into a mans premises or house. Can't say whether this was from fear or hatred of the people. This last trate was not regretted by any one. So matters wears on about this way up to.

January 15, 1863

By January 15, 1863, we are now having rain and sleet with it. The water courses very high. Our streets now have the look of a wagon yard, being crowded nearly all the time with going and returning trains from Nashville with army provisions—being no R. Road in operation. The bridges all destroyed. Round the town was full of camps of soldiers. In the day time a perfect croud—now and then one citizen would seem as by accident to find another among the croud of soldiers.

There were many citizens who had left their houses when Bragg retreated. Could take but little with them, left the houses locked up by those who could not get some one to take the place, thinking nothing would be molested. They will be wofully disappointed if ever they get back. These houses were not long unoccupied for the soldiers made convenient to occupy, and for fuel would make use of fences and out houses, use furniture, and if they wished to occupy another place would take what suited along with them.

January 20, 1863

Very little improvement for the last week. Things getting more settled, but wood and provisions running short. It did begin to look as though want was about to stare us in the face, but better chance for help. But it did seem that providence by some way caused provision to be made for the necessary wants. Wood did come and provision also. To take a view of matters about this time, one could not help asking the question—how did they get along, not having vehicles for hauling, or passes to go out of the lines?

A system of improving hospitals now commenced and rooms for army stores. All the business houses were being occupied. Many of them had been finished, at considerable cost by the owners, with counters and shelving. These were moved and piled on side walks, lay there until they gradually disappeared, either to burn or to use. The rooms, now being clear, they were either filled with bunks for the wounded soldiers or filled with army stores or a post commisisions. Trains of wagons filled with armed soldiers are still on the go, foraging on the farmers for corn, fodder and large loads of cedar rails for fuel. Poltry and every thing of the kind had to bear a part in these forage excursions. Should the owner at these times expostulate, would get but little satisfaction and most generally some impudent abuse in return. This is now a daily business.

When out on these expeditions they would be tampering with the negros on the plantations, telling them they were as free as their masters; that if they did work, should have the pay for it. Give them to understand if they would come to the camps they would pay them from ten to fifteen dollars (which was as much as they were getting themselves). This was an inducement to have the negro run off.

January 25, 1863

At a loss to know what is to become of the people. They are now greatly troubled with anoyances continually. It does appear to be an appendex to Pharoahs troubles or plagues. There is scarcely a hole or corner but what a Yankee head or hand is thrust into it in search of riches, for there are many of them think that every body in the south is rich or has money from their action in the matter. It does seem there are numbers of them that would be willing to grabble in a s-t house if they were satisfied they would find a five cent piece by so doing.

Such is their great love of money.

February 1, 1863

The federal army continues to come in this place, in great numbers—foraging going on in a regular way. They have got them selves pretty well settled in their quarters. A good many houses has been **burned**, in the out skirts of town and the neighboring portions of the county. Other have been pulled down for various purposes by the army. If it should be continued any length of time, and become a general thing, it will take the country a long time to recover from the effect. So much property melting away - every week, of every species.

Skirmishing parties are sent out every day, but they appear to effect but little in their trips.

After these fellows get through with the negros, that is, offering them pay for their time and rations, they then commence enquiring about the master. First, is he a 'sesesh,' or union man, has he got much **money**, is he rich? Make enquiry about the quantity of stock. Has he any thing **hid** and where. All these questions are answered, quite promptly by the contraband as they are now called. The Yankees are disposed to believe the negros as to the truth of a thing sooner than they will a white man. They claim the negro to be their best friend.

The negros now begin to shew an indifference about home. When an order is given them to do any thing, they go at it in a slow, careless manner. Begin to be impudent and contrary. The next news we hear he, or she, is off at some head quarters as they call it. They have made an arrangement with some officer to wait on him at a price stipulated and when there can give a great deal of reliable information, and from it arrests can and is made of some one—how is this? Why, we get it from an intelligent, reliable contraband.

Well, let the devils go. They are now not worth the fire they warm by. Shall likely refer often of their doings in course of notes of the times, for the present stop.

February 15, 1863

About this time, Feb. 15, 1863, preparation is being made for building fortifications and rifle pits near this place. Large quantities of timber trees are cut and hauled to the grounds. The work is commenced and pushed on rigerously - digging and blasting rocks. A great number of negros are employed at this kind of work, **under pay**, of course.

The works lie over a large tract of land, owned by Lytle and Murfree, bordering on Stones River at the R. Road crossing. They are also constructing what they call field hospitals. For materials of this, go to town and when find one story houses, without further ceremony commence pulling it down and haul off before the owners face, never once saying with your leave, but on the contrary, a little impudance. Such as he, is a d-d "sesesh" and ought not have a house. Such is power—it can tyranize over weakness.

Now, the building of fortifications at this place does not look like a waste of time and money. They will scarcely ever have an opportunity of firing a gun at an enemy at this place, but military men probably know the best.

The confederates are occupying Shelbyville and through the country this side. Now and then, a slight skirmishing takes place between squads of cavalry, without any thing of consequence being done at these times.

Can hear of little being done, by either army, in any quarter. All having the appearance of being quiet in **front**, as the term is now generally used, among the soldiers.

The wounded, at this place are in a better condition and are improving. Comparatively but fiew die. Such as can be removed with convenience are sent off. This brings dates up to about Feb. 22, 1863.

February 22, 1863

By February of 1863 the Forts, being now far advanced in construction, guns were mounted at their proper places and things began to assume the appearance of defence.

This being Washingtons birth day was thought proper to celebrate the day by firing **Thirty four** guns, one for each state, whether in or out of the union. With the exception of this, things had the appearance of quietness here.

The Confederate Army, a portion having fallen back to Tullahoma, still occupying Shelbyville and other parts in the vicinity. Their pickets or cavalry would venture sometimes within five miles of this place. Nothing would transpire, of importance, from these near visits. There has been a great deal of rain fallen lately. The Cumberland river is now in good boating order. The Federals are rushing large quantities of army stores to Nashville before the fall.

March 1, 1863

Things much as they have been for some time past. The forts still progressing in their work and foraging business **more** so. The country for several miles round has been striped of every thing that can possibly be spared, leaving many with very short allowance to subsist on.—

Large numbers of cavalry and infantry passing out and in every fiew days. They have procured a **Pontoon Bridge**, which is hauled out for the purpose of crossing Stones River. On the road leading to Lebanon can hear of many Confed. prisoners being captured and coming in every day and giving themselves up. So say the Yankees. Now if this is the case, the thing is done very quiet for none are seen in Murfreesboro.

The Negros are leaving their homes and coming to town every day. They are seen with a bundle of cloths on their heads and shoulders, **marching in** to obtain their freedom. They are getting more worthless and impudent. Their idea of freedom is to be free, be clothed, and do nothing either for themselves or any body else. Steal as a matter of course. Speak to any of the Yankees of letting them be free and go North to live. To that they object, swear they shall not cross the Ohio river. They don't want them there—poor, deluded negro. Your fate will be a hard one.

Refugees

There is a large number of country people, from different sections, that has congregated here. That is commonly called **refugees**, who, as a class of people, are generally a degree below the negro, but, like the negro, make their appearance. Man and woman, half clad, with a half doz tow head children, all with small bundles under their arms of old quilts and a fiew articles of clothing. Another set—a man carrying a bundle, which appears to be about the house hold for himself, wife, and three or four tow heads and a dog or two. His elbows and knees out, a seedy hat, and an apology for shoes, wife half clothed and looked like she had not been near water for a month or more. Children frequently barefooted, hair resembling porcupine quills.

These motly crouds make their appearance, tell a pitiful tale, say that every thing they had was taken from them. It is plainly seen, they had nothing to take. They, like the negro, came here to be fed and do nothing, as usual.

These people claimed to call themselves **Union, came** for **protection**. Some of them thought the "sesesh" ought to be turned out of their house and let them have the places to live. These people lay, or camped, in the Baptist church, men, women, and children.

Their friends, the Yankees, did not have much confidence in them. They allowed the men to carry their wood on their shoulders for half mile without offering to haul. Had to cook out in the street. Many of these men were put on the fortifications to work for rations. This may be a hard set picture to look. **It is** the truth.

There was a little better looking class of **Union** men, who run off from the rebel lines, left their families at home to take care of themselves as best they may. They did not wish to be conscripted, thought this to be a more safe place. But the Yankees, always a calculating people, thought there was too many **good soldiers** out of the army, so they set about and formed a regiment, as far as it would go, out of this stock. No doubt but there was many a disappointed fellow "Out of the frying pan into the fire."

House Search

Among other things going on with the Yankees, it was thought necessary to search citizen houses, for what, cant tell. They said, for arms and amunition or army stores. Thus, a corporal and four men would go to a house, half on each side, to prevent any escape, meet in family room. What do you wish here? "We are ordered to search your house."

They are conducted from one room to another by one of the family—open drawers, boxes, and trunks, turn up the articles that is in them - examine all corners, in the pantry, smoke house, turn up the meat that is in boxes. In fact, no place escapes a look and that done by who? If they were at home, it could be told.

At some of these places of search, a watch would disappear from its place of hanging and other small articles of value would go to keep it company. In these searches, a hundred little circumstances would take place—some of a verry singular character, such as wanting to read letters and things of that kind.

The main object, it was subsequently understood, was to find any stores that Gen. Bragg may have left behind, but the above was done as an extra matter to pick up small articles of value and put that in their own pockets. They believe the people of the south are all rich.

At this time, great preparation is being made for an assault on Vicksburg. The general impression is, if it should fall into the Federal hands, the Rebel army would have to dry up, as they are getting large supplys from Texas, and that would be cut off.

As to that, it is all supposition. They have other places that will furnish them. Every part of the southern country produces well. Where cotton will grow any thing else will. As for starving the south, it is only talking idly.

March 5, 1863

There is very good order kept about the streeds. Guards about the corners. Soldiers generally kept close in their quarters, not allowed to visit about citizens houses as they were wont to do the last year. They may have some policy in so doing. The fear may be, the soldiers might be induced to become rebels to their cause, as they are a motly compound, at best. However, the order suits well all round.

This may now be claimed to be a city of distinction in point of populations, including the subburbs of about forty five thousand inhabitants, generally of a **blue cast** and smartly touched with **Black**.

The large class dwelling houses are now occupied as head quarters for officers and negros. Several of them have been vacated by the owners who had gone south, leaving their furniture locked up.

Many of these officers had women who had followed along with the army. These they called **wives**, possibly some of them were, but some of them had been raised without the advice of a good mother from actions and appearances.

Slang Words

As a matter of curiosity, will here insert a fiew Yankee slang words, that is frequently used by them, in conversations and otherwise.

Skedaddled — To run away, or, disperse from. The word is often applied to the Rebels. When the Yankees thought there was no danger of catching up with them, "they skedaddled so!" They are afraid to stand and fight.

Gobbled — Means to steal small articles of value from the rebels such as books, pictures, and any fancy articls. Drs and wives, second rate officers and wives, and a fiew **Persons**, will not hesitate to gobble up.

Smavelled — To catch a rebel soldier suddenly, unexpected to him.

Mug You — To choke his adversary black in the face, then let him go with a kick.

Copperhead — A war politician, who is disposed for peace on any terms, willing to cut loose from the southern states and let them go.

Shebang — A small place to do business in and but little in it - a small office. Come in, this is my Shebang!

Galvanized Rebel — One that has been forced to take oath against his better judgement. The Yankees doubt his loyalty.

Iron Clad — One who has taken the oath, for form sake, but does not have much confidence in the strength of it. Nearly the same as "galvanized." The Yankees fear to trust them.

Green Back — A species of money (paper), used by the Federal government, issued for war purposes. Takes its name from the back of all the notes, being covered with heavy engraving and printed with green ink.

Guerrilla — A name given to all confederate cavalry men by the Yankee.

Bush Whacker — Men that lie concealed, in ambush, and kills his adversary. They are dreaded much by the Yankees.

Intelligent Contraband — A run away negro, who can work upon the cedulity of a Yankee, who will take his word as soon as he will a white mans oath.

Union Man — (Modern), one that takes pleasure in destroying property of the "sesesh." Will take horses and stock of any kind, forage generally and call it pressing, burn houses and fences. Put his hand in your pocket, take your watch and money. A restorer of the constitution of the U. States—a leveller.

Sesesh — Are what the Yankees call rebels to the U.S. A class of soldiers. They are continually on the hunt of but are cautious of coming up with or of finding them.

Bully For You? — A Yankee word - that is, if you say or do a smart thing as they think, express satisfaction, saying "bully for?"

All Right! — A word when things are ready or suits - go ahead - used by Southern.

Spondulicks — A word used for ready cash, as, I have or have none, of the S—s.

Butter Nut — Designated for the color of clothing the confederate soldier wears, being wollen jeanes, dyed brown, with walnut, or butter nut bark.

Gray Back — A species of currency, gotten up for war purpose by the Confederate government, on the same principle as that of the U S. Also a name given to the confed. soldier, their uniform being gray cloth.

That's The Trouble — When a thing pleases, or not, much used by the Yankee soldiers. Not much point in the expression.

Expression

The Federal army, having now occupied this place about two months, not much business to occupy their time, are shewing wrestlessness. Many of them when they get an opportunity of conversation with a citizen, when they think there will be no impropriety will express their feelings, freely come out and say that they are not pleased with the Lincoln administration. When they first volunteered, it was to sustain the union. They undertook to fight, but from appearances there is too much of the negro getting mixed up in the thing, and if they had the power they would lay down their guns tomorrow and go home. Others would say, I came to fight for the union as it was, but it begins to look to me that this war is nothing more than a mob, did not expect to fight for the liberation of the Negro. While others will dam them and wish they were in the ocean. They shall not cross the Ohio river to go in their country.

But, there are always two sides to every thing. We find a large number who are for freeing, or rather argue that it would be better the negros were free. They contend they are human beings and as such ought to be free.

Such is about the general feeling through the union army. One can gather enough to see how the thing is about to work. The devil is behind the curtain. His foot can be seen from under his blankets. He and his emissarys (abolitionist), are about getting up a good thing in their way. They are moving things gently at the present time.

The officers are acting their part, not so much for the restoration of the union, for many of them don't care whether it is ever restored. The longer the war lasts, the better for them to line their pockets with money, for at this business they are getting good wages. Stop it, they are thrown out of employment, and of course it is to their interest to keep the rebellion on hand as long as possible.

This is about the **gist** of the patriotism of the majority of them. They are using great exertion to shew the people at home through their glowing corrispondence, that the soldiers are all well satisfied with their situation in the army and are determined to crush out the rebellion or die in the attempt. Now this is a thing said for them. They are not permitted to speak out their real sentiments.

The soldiers sentiments are Thirteen dollars and hard tack (bread), and fighting for the liberation of the negroes. No compensation to me, to be deprived of my family and enduring the hardships of the camps.

Should the officers hear these poor fellows, would likely for this, treason. Have to carry a headless barrel with his head out at the top, or a rail for two or three hours on his shoulders, for two or three days, or be tied up by the thumbs, over his head - as such are their punishments in camps.

It is with the soldier in camp, like politics. They are governed by public or camp sentiment, not their own will but that of their leaders.

Only a certain kind of newspaper is permitted to be distributed in camps among soldiers. They must be the "Simon pure," or they are forbid. Those that come near the truth, and not touch, is the kind that the soldier may read. All other is contraband.

As we have been on the subject of officers and men, will presume it may not be out of place to say a little more about them. There are among this class of gentry here **women** purporting to be wives of officers - but, from the conduct of many of them, leaves reason of doubt. An army is not a place for a female of proper or refined feelings. When we see a woman wearing long ringlets, large ear trinkets, a flowing feather in her hat, galloping up and down over the country with officers and soldiers, having oyster suppers and wine drinking, it may be set down she does not not lie at the feet of **Boaz** for nothing. Such we see here. Perhaps there were some that were genuine wives, that made their visits to the army. The majority were of the former description. A Lady or Gentleman can always be known in any situation they may be placed, and so may the other class be as easily distinguished. In either case, it does not require a keen observer to see the difference.

This officer goes to one of the best citizens house, walks in looks round the rooms, says to owner, "I wish to occupy two rooms." "Cant well spare it." "Compelled to have it." May be parlour sitting room or the best rooms up stairs - leaves. In a short time he and friend and their **wives** return. Have servants with them - if not, order owners servants - promise to pay them high wages. By so doing, they occupy the whole time to inconvenience of the owner.

The rooms, is of course, furnished. They and their wives make themselves at home. Order as they please. If table ware is needed - send servant for it. If any get broke or lost - make no apology. Verry little care taken of any thing in the rooms. Cook and litter the premises - no difference. We are allowed to subsist on the rebels. Pass and repass the man or woman of the house, do not pretend to see them. They have their wine, oysters, and confections. Visitors and servants trotting up and down stairs at almost all hours of night - get mellow, jump on the floor, like they were trying to go through. Remain at this place a month or so and leave, frequently without saying - I am obliged to you for the use of your rooms. These are colns. of some regiment.

Now, make some enquiry of some of the members of col. regiment, whom we have made a friendly acquaintance. Soldier - who is Col. A. What business did he follow at home? Well! Sir, I have seen him frequently in... He was following the business as tapster to a **soda fount** at a drinking saloon. He was a talking sort of a fellow. Quite a would-be politician. Was disposed to put on **airs**. Was not thought of otherwise much of a man.

Col. D. - I knew him also. He did little or nothing. It is said played cards and billiards. Would run in debt for his board and clothing and scarcely paid any body. Could tell good jokes and was pretty well liked as a man. Was popular with the common crouds. When the war broke out was one of the first to propose the getting up of a volunteer company.

Such is a sample of officers that we find in the Yankee army, with a fiew exceptions. Such men are making the war more a speculation than for the restoration of the Union. Such men, politically, call themselves **Democrats** - and, such we find in both armys. Their policy has been to rule or ruin.

March 10, 1863

Hear but little of the doings of the army of the Potomac, or other quarters. Now and then a move is said to be made, more to keep up an excitement than any thing else.

The Federal army that is stationed at Franklin and Spring Hill, Ten., are quite annoyed by the Rebel Cavalry. Occasionally heavy skirmishing takes place between the parties. The Federal lost a great many prisoners taken at these places by Gen. Van Dorn.

The roads improving about this time, and a move of Gen. Rosecrans is anticipated to the front. The wounded that is in the hospitals are improving fast, and as they are in a condition, are sent off immediately.

March 15, 1863

By March of 1863 the Federal army has been distributed out in different portions of the county at Cripple Creek, Readyville, Woodbury, and McMinnville. At all these places quite heavy forces were stationed.

Matters were quiet with the exception of now and then slight skirmishing would take place. No damage done at these times, though verry heavy forces of Federal Cavalry were all the time on the go. Whether they were particular to find any thing to fight in this rounds is a question. The fortifications here is still progressing.

Now, commencing what is called field hospitals. And for material—come to town and pull down small frame houses and haul off, not particular whose property it is. Just as soon order a man out as any other way. Not certain that some such cases did happen. A red headed and red whiskered fellow with a mark of a hammer and hatchet on his coat sleeve, who was called pioneer, would ride round hunting houses that would suit. If any objection should be made, get nothing in return but impudent talk. Order his men to pull down house and move off. Number of houses were destroyed in this way.

The soldiers were in the habit of pulling off plank from houses and fences to make floors in their tents. Cedar log houses, stables, and fence picketing would be carried to camps for fire wood. Almost impossible to keep them from it. Was a general annoyance that had to be submitted to. A great deal was done, as a matter of contempt for "Sesesh" people.

The Pro. Vost. was verry stringent about giving passes to citizens or allowing them to trade. Every fiew days, new orders would be out.

We had frequent changes of Prov. Vo. Marshals. Did appear that each one would try to improve in his rigor on the citizens. Orders given that citizens shall not buy beef or other articles without taking the oath. Many would avail themselves of the said oath, which was against the will. Others would still hold out against it, but all did more or less make some friend among the common soldier. They would procure articles in small quantities from the commissary or by their savings at camp and sell at government price to citizens. It did sometimes look like stealing, the way the matter had to be managed. Had to promise soldier not to mention any thing about their letting persons have any thing.

At this time, the army were receiving large droves beef cattle. Some of them were fine looking, others had to be killed soon, to keep them from dying. They were generally kept in lots in and about town. It took about fifty or sixty every day to supply the demand of the army and hospitals. They would drive out that number, shoot them down. When butchered, it generally covered over a half acre ground, the entrils, heads and feet, left lying there—so in the course of time several acres was covered in this way, and it began to get warm weather. The smell became very offensive.

We began to be apprehensive that it would cause sickness, but as fortune would have it, the authorities took the matter in hand—dug pits, had the offensive collected up and thrown in and covered up. This caused the atmosphere to improve. Large numbers horses died and were lying round in the neighborhood. They, too, were disposed of in a similar manner and in a short time the whole nuisance was finally abated. Large numbers horses were shot, such as were very poor, diseased and woarn out. Here was a fortune lost to some speculating, enterprising Yankee, in the way of sculls, horns and shin bones.

A system of street cleaning now commenced. Hands were set to work scraping up all the litter that was lying in the streets, gutters and corners, hauled out town. Things now begin to put on a more cheerful and healthy appearance, but still depradations would be made by soldiers on fences around garden lots. Plank off out houses, flooring and windows would all gradually disappear, until finally, none would be left—this to fix their tents; brick, for making chimneys. One set would destroy in this way. About the time they were done fixing, orders would come to move to some other quarter. All this work would be left. It would then be pulled down by the negros and carried off for fuel.

In a short time, a new set soldiers comes in. The same process is gone through. So it will be seen - pull down - build up - to pull down and burn. Such is the doings with the soldiers and negros.

If it is the wish to save a fence from destruction, should a plank or picket be pulled off, must go and replace one immediately, or it will soon go "because, some one else had done it before them." This is the sterotype excuse of all.

Justice!

While the confederate army were here, they had killed a great number of beef cattle for the use of the army, had not sent off the hides. The Federal army came. They, of course, were the owner, being captured property. However, these hides were said to be sold to some Cincinati Tanner. Be this as it may—when the purchaser took them off, they also pretended to have orders. Went to the Tanyards of this place, took all that was in or out the vats with them. This was private property. Without paying a dime for the leather, or giving any further satisfaction about the matter. Owner did not know who to apply to, and, of course, was given up as a loss.

It can be seen how easy to steal when a person has a mind to and not be found out. Should they be caught in the act, does not amount to any thing. "tis all from the d-d Sesesh." This is not an isolated case, but one of scores, that is happening every day. Property of every description goes in this way making **thieves rich** at the **expense of honest men**.

Negros

The negros or "inteligent contrabands," as they are called, or more proper, "colored men," are making their appearance within the lines more frequent, bringing with them bundles of clothing. When they arrive, generally have a fine tale to tell. Of course, badly abused at home. Come for protection. Heard to say "I tole em all, and tole em good too! - how da did - did'nt giv me notin to eat."

In consequence of the requirements of the oath, or be put through the lines, many of the citizens availed themselves of the latter course. They took the road south.

There were quite a number that left their homes here, vacated. They disposed of their property among their friends for safe keeping, much as conveniently. A large portion left in their houses, locked up, as they think to remain these **honest times**, unmolested. We shall see what becomes of it in the course of time.

March 20, 1863

Genl. Bragg's army is lying in and about the neighborhood of Shelbyville. His army is filled with men of much the same material as armys generally are. A good many reckless young men in it and, for the want of better employment, are manufacturing mischief, for the amusement of themselves and others. Will note a case or two of soldiers tricks while in the camps there. Among the lot, there was one, in particular—

David Sly

David Sly, "a devil may catch me" sort of a fellow, who loved a good joke and a little whiskey better. He makes a plan, how whiskey can be got. To get through the lines was a thing to be managed. He and one of his friends, at night, slip close to where the pickets are posted—for the purpose of getting the watch word. They did not have to wait long in their hiding place before an officer came by. He, of course, knew and gave it. They now, in possession, slip out of the hiding place, come boldly to the pickets, give the word and pass in town. By next morning, arrangements are made for robbing the commissary store. Enough had been put in the secret, to carry out the plan. Thus, about a quarter of an hour before the relief was to come on, the number necessary for guard procured guns, approached those that were on picket at the commissary. Sly, acting as corporal, sings out "**Rebel guard**." They take their place. The guard march off and leave them. No sooner than they are out of sight, the bogus guard go in the house and hand out what they want the back way - leave soon as possible with their prize. When the proper guard arrive to relieve, no one to be found - empty shelves - whiskey all gone.

Sly At Another Time

Puts one of guard in guard house. In strolling along the streets, Sly is picked up by a couple who are on guard duty. Start off with him to guard house. In going on, he makes it convenient to stump his toe, severely, falls down, appearantly in great pain. Cant get along, lies there, unable to walk. One of the guard proposes going to camp to get something to relieve him. The other remains. While they are by themselves, asks guard to let him see his gun. Takes hold - rises to his feet - give the order **March!** Now, takes guard prisoner to guard house, under protest. He remonstrates. They wont hear his tale. Has to submit. Sly now manages to leave his gun, and return back. Meets the other guard from camp, says to him, "I have been there, they have discharged me" - passes on about his business.

March 25, 1863

On March 25, 1863, skirmishing continues about over the country and in the neighborhood. The cavalry forces meet at Milton, Ten. Had a close engagement for a short time. Some fiew Feds wounded. They brought a small number prisoners back, did not understand what damage was done to the confed. side.

Churches Cleared

Two or three of the churches have been cleared of the wounded, having been used as hospitals. They were cleaned and seats replaced and ready for church service. This bring the first opportunity for a thing of the kind for three months past.

It does seem we are falling back in the dark ages. The prospect does not brighten much. Things gloomy. Possibly we are in the dark hours just before day. We could complain, if it would avail anything toward the relief of our troubles. But we are doomed. We must suffer on. How long? The answer is in futurity — but, what use of moralizing at such times as these? The same scenes have been gone through often, and possibly greater distress, than we are realizing. Job had his troubles yet he had his comforts. May we not anticipate happiness in a future place?

Contrabands are coming in, more numerous. They begin to shew good deal impudence. are disposed to take liberty whether allowed them or not - men, women and children all alike in this respect.

A fiew days since a stout, negro fellow raised a brick bat to strike a citizen in his own yard because he had been forbid the privilege of getting water there. Verrily, things are comeing to a fine pass. Well! (Sore heads) predicted.

Army matters much at a stand still. Some talk about making a move from here to the front. There is an attact anticipated on Vicksburg in a short time. Likely delay may be made to see what the result will be as one branch of an army governs another.

A Move To The Fortifications

The fortifications having now been so far advanced toward completion that the soldiers can occupy. Quite a move of soldiers and army stores at this time is taking place to the new fortification. Artillery and every thing of the kind. This move causes the vacation of many of the business houses round the public square which has been filled to overflowing.

There is some skirmishing with the cavalry going on about the neighborhood of Readyville and other places in that section - no body hurt.

The Federals are anticipating an attact at this place, but why they should is rather an absurd idea. Their fears are groundless.

The rebels are too well posted as to the position to be caught in the trap that is set for them. They are, generally, well acquainted with the localities of Murfreesboro and vicinity. Another thing, they would not hazzard the life of the citizens by making an attact on this place. If they have to wait for a rebel army to come to their fortifications, it may be a long time before they will get an opportunity to fire their guns from the forts.

Among other buildings at the forts - a large Depot at the river. This is for storage of army materials, and stores. Are also busy hauling in the farmers out houses and stables to put up at the forts, but most likely to **burn** and destroy. In this way, as it seems, that their bent is more on destruction than any thing else.

The Exodus of negros continues to increase, comeing to the promised land. All sorts, old and young, halt and almost blind, lugging in their small estates on their heads and sholders.

April 1, 1863

Every thing now quite dull, skirmishers are sent out in different directions every day. It has the appearance of great waste of time. Still working on the fortifications. No news of importance, citizens walking about the streets and are seen sitting in small groups whitling sticks and smoking.

Several citizens brought in from the country on some frivolous charge are not permitted to leave for home. The prospect bad for their making a crop this season. The weather dry and the roads in good order for traveling purposes. The Federal army have contemplated a move for some time, but from cause are here yet. The patients in the hospitals are recovering fast.

April 5, 1863

To day we part with our patient, Ajt. Burk, of the Confederate army. Having now been with us for three months past, he has, so far, recovered that it is necessary now to send him forward, a prisoner of war. His wound, which was in the foot, is far from being well. His suffering was great in consequence. He bore it with patience.

April 15, 1863

Find things much after the same manner as the last date. No more of the army in any direction, still in expectation of doing so in a short time. The cavalry still galloping over the country, the result not much. The wounded are recovering fast. As they are able to do duty, are sent to their commands.

The Confederate soldiers are now so far recovered. They are all sent off for exchange. The hospitals are now, in a manner, clear of all wounded and sick soldiers - things quiet.

The news papers continue to keep up the excitement by Telegraph dispatches. There is little confidence placed in them. It is more to sell papers than any thing else.

The general health of this place may be said to be good. Our streets are crouded every day with soldiers. It is now the citizens who may be called strangers, only now and then they meet each other.

Quite a trade is now going on in the way of selling apples among the soldiers. They do things up in a city style, open shop any place on the street. Have a good run of costom as long as a barrel apples last.

April 20, 1863

Numbers of the Federal army are disposed to think that they will be attact at this place by Gen. Bragg, but this is certainly a grounalys fear. They send out large detachments of infantry in different directions. They generally bring back good reports of their operation, but it does seem they are better on reports than they are in finding the army.

They have collected a number of citizens from the country, arrested under various charges but really of no importance. Are retaining them more to shake them loose from making a crop. Appear to have nothing against them. Have seen over forty men in attendance at the Pro Vost Marshals office about nine of mornings to answer to their names, then are dismissed until the next morning.

The balance of the time they have to amuse themselves by whittling sticks, smoking, reading the papers, discussing war news, walking about and when the Grape Vine will work have some exciting Telegrams for discussion. Thus the day wears off.

April 25, 1863

A further report of the completion of the fortification works and occupation.

The next thing to be done is to clear out the timber for some distance all round the works. Now in the immediate vicinity of Murfreesboro, the land is covered with large bodies of fine timber. The owners sustained great loss by the destruction of the woodland.

The fortifications lie about a half to three fourths of a mile north of Murfreesboro, on the road leading to Nashville by the pike, are principly on the land of W.F. Lytle. His land extends from the Lebanon pike on the north to the Shelbyville pike south, meandering with the river, most generally heavy timbered. Jno. Bell Jr. adjoining near town. Chas. Ready, D. Maney, L.H. Carney, R. Currins and parts of several other tracts all together in a body. This is all in the fort range, all ordered to be cut down without reserve to owner. We can now see for miles in some direction from town. Ready, Bell, Murfree and Carneys farm houses are entirely destroyed and portions of numbers of others.

Things are so changed that in the course of time it will be a hard matter to trace out the original land marks. A wilderness of timber has disappeared and in its place a large prairie waste.

At this time there is quite a mania with officers of all grades and others having small desks, small boxes, walking canes, crutches, etc. made of cedar. Said to have come off the Stones River battle ground. These things are manufactured and sent home as mementos of their chivaldry at the Stones River battle. Fence plank and cedar rails suffered for this business. Cedar was a popular growth with the Yankees and they sawed many a hole in their jackets.

May 1, 1863

Every thing appears to be in a state of quietness, not much doing in the way of business. The soldiers have more disposition to trade than to look out for a fight. They are most generally in the apple trade.

Apples sell as high as twenty eight dollars for barrel. At this price they buy and sell at a profit. The Yankees, as has been remarked, are great eaters, notwithstanding their great love of money will pay high prices for apples or any thing else to eat.

Some of them had a mode of extracting money out of Uncle Sam's pocket. There were many little squads of negros divided out to work on different departments of labor, a white man to oversee them. This man is permitted to draw rations for them, generally a week's allowance. Of this he would deal out to them in less quantities, retain the balance and report more hands than he had, so each week would have a good surplus on hand. This, of course, would go in his own pocket.

The commissary men were not allowed to sell to any person without order, but when no one was about but customer, a trade was made. This, of course, retired in his pocket. So every thing went. Every one that had an office, no matter what discription, it was made to pay. May suppose that is what large numbers came in the army for. Enter a poor man and come out in good circumstances.

Every branch of officers of all descriptions make money. The soldier is the only one that has no chance to put his hand in the government pocket. They have to make up their stealings from citizenry property and they are quite expert at that branch. No harm with them, when out foraging, to take a citizens horse and sell it. It is hard to tell who did it as one will not inform on another.

As armys are made up of a variety of characters will introduce two or three other descriptions, and sorry to have it to say, in a great number of cases, perfect impositions in their way. They are not fit to fill the places at home much less in the camp.

Physicians and Surgeons

As seen at hospitals. They, as a body of men in their capacity, should be of the first class in knowledge of their art, but the contrary many would not make a respectable horse doctor. Whiskey heads, this is the sort that is allowed to tamper with the lives of men, by experementing on them. If patient die, it would be a matter of course.

To go on with the story, these life preservers would occaisionally walk round among the patients in the hospitals, prescribe in a careless way, to nurse say what ought or may be done, pass off to his room or some where else, the last that is likely seen of him that day. If any little delicacy sent in by some friend to the sick, would be left with the head doctor. It frequently never got further, probably the health of patient would not bear it, eat it for him. Liquors that were stimulants was used generally by the Doctors and friends, patients too weak, it would likely effect their heads, drink it for them. Thus it goes.

By evening our Drs are in a reclining way, having to take so many prescriptions for the sick. They are laid up a fiew days from the effect. From the look of face, one would suppose they had a very dangerous fever.

It must not be understood that this is the case with all, speak only of the majority of the so called sirgeons found at hospitals who took that place for the reason they are not worthy of patronage at home, but must subsist on.

Thus there are some at hospitals, and well there are, that are high tone gentlemen, well qualified to fill that or any other station who would scorn to do a low mean thing.

Cooks

The cooks, in many instances, came in for a share on the same list for grievances in their line of business. They have a nack of taking care of No. 1 under the old addage "that it is a poor cook that will starve."

So it is they eat the best and fix up something for the sick. If they can't eat, it is their own fault. It is not expected that a hospital would be much of a place to have delicacies for the sick, but such as they have could be prepared in a better manner than it generally is.

Don't wonder that persons are so much opposed going to hospitals, particularly if they have once been inmates of sick place.

Preachers

And there is introduced another class of men in the shape of Preachers. Numbers of them join the army as chaplins for the morals and good of souls of the soldiers. They in a common way may be good men when they first enter, but being in the army, exposed to all weathers, soon learn to take morning dram for the preservation of health, enter into many other little vices of the camp. They begin to neglect religious duties, dont preach often. When they do soldier has little confidence in them as religious men. They see these christian professors are no better than they should be. They soon begin to loose weight with the army, generally are going step by step. These men, in their progress, are showing a disposition, if possible, to deceive their God, themselves they do deceive. The devil being an arch manager has determined to have his share of thses divines, possibly he may have been enlarging his domains for the last fiew years for the in coming immigration.

Fears are entertained that the devil has employed this class of men as emmissaries in the great work of the rebellion. The preachers, North and South, seems to have a tendency that way. Instance — Before the war broke out there were a class of christians called Methodist, who divided themselves in two parties, the one called the Northern, the other Southern Methodist. These two parties at one time had heavy skirmishing and came to a close engagement on paper. The South carried the point of contention and a division was the consequence.

This difficulty originated about a claim on the decendance of Ham, one for freeing, the other for holding them in bondage. After the defeat the matter still lay broiling until the present time. The North felt disposed to renew the attact. The gauntlet was thrown. South accepted it. Thus, the war.

As the war was now about to assume a different form, Methodist preachers felt patriotic and anxious to enter the contest and the majority of them imagined they were qualified for officers of some sort, boldly enrolled their names and made application for a situation as commander. Such as could not get appointment accepted the place of Chaplin to the army until a vacancy should occur. Fiew felt humble enough to enter the ranks as a common Soldier.

Now hear of Generals who are preachers. They have hung up their religion on a nail, for the present and entered the field to win glory and renown and praise of men. And there is our pious chaplin who has had an opportunity to advance. He was known in early days to be one of the most pious and one of the greatest revivalists in all the country, appearantly did much good in his way, made vows that he would devote his time to the service of his Lord to the neglect of all other business.

Alas! How do we find him? See him addicted to taking bitters pretty regular for his health, with some in his pocket, occaisionally flourishing it to the eminet danger of the company he is in.

The last account was said to be in E. Tennessee raising a regiment and ranking as Colonel. Would not say that he could swear a modest, handsome oath, possibly can graze it close without touching.

This is a slight picture of a Southern diciple who has entered the army for the glory of men. It applys to many.

Again we have a man who has entered the army as chaplin. He leaves his friends and home and little flock of confiding christians to take care of themselves as best they can, to enter in the great cause of the redemption of down trodden and oppressed sons of Ham, on his way shouting liberty and union.

Where do we next find this christian patriot? Away down south in some populous town or city, having almost neglected his calling as chaplin, question arises what is he doing. He has managed to get the agency for collecting up the property of what is termed "abandoned," that is house, furniture, books and articles generally that has been deposited by citizens with their friends and they gone south. This he finds out by "inteligent contrabands," goes and calls for in the name of the U.S. government. This property is gathered at one place, under the plea that it is Rebel property and confiscated, will be condemned and sold. The truth is the U. States will never lay its finger on much of the proceeds of sales. This christian friend came to the army for the purpose of making money and to do so has turned to down right stealing.

This is a miniature of a Northern chaplin. His idea does not run so high in the scale of greatness, but his capacity is as great as the Southern chaplin. The one seems to attain to military glory, the other glorys in devilish thieving.

Now see their master standing by smileing approvingly, patting them on the shoulder, exclaiming well done good and faithful servants, I will reward the openly.

His Satanic magisty is well pleased with his success in operating with this class of christian, no doubt he will be true to his promise of reward.

Hospitals

Next go to hospitals, look round for chaplin that was supposed to have been retained for the purpose of administering religious comfort and advice to the sick and wounded soldier. Question asked and response, all gone to the "front" with the army where they would have less trouble and a better opportunity of being promoted to a more profitable situation.

"Sodom" will not be destroyed yet. Find one private at eleven dollars a month who is in the capacity of nurse. Can scarcely read but he willingly offers his servises. He attends to the patients, administers instruction, prays and preaches, or exhorts in the different wards to the best of his ability and is doing some good.

Incident

While on this subject, will relate a circumstance. Strolling along the streets in a meditative mood in the out skirts of town, meet a gentlemanly looking man. It being a pleasant day, we stop and get in conversation on different topics. Seeing I was a citizen, asked me if I had been here long. Satisfied him on that point, then asked him if he was a Soldier, he being some what dressed in that style. Answer no, he was out in the capacity of chaplin to some regiment, nameing it was from one of the Northern states. He did not happen to be a Methodist, but said his doctrine was rather on that order.

During the conversation he remarked there was a division in the army camping not far from him which was from the North. It had about Seventy Methodist preachers of all grades, officers (good God!) and two or three regiments that more than two thirds were members of that church, was called Methodist Division. The thought occurred - Here is a field for work. The old fellow will have his hands full for a while.

U.S. Christian Commission

There is another religious office created for the purpose of making money, filled by any denomination, generally by some old man who is likely not able to support himself at home. To wit, the U.S. Christian Commission. Its business is to destribute tracts, books and papers to soldiers and others. The object may be a good one but the gist of the thing is to amass a fiew Green Backs.

One of this kind of officer was opened in the parlour of F. Henry for a while, against his consent, and occupied by one or two middle age Saints and about the same number of Angelic forms who glided about the premises as matrons or something else. They cooked, they eat, they sleep and they —— all in this christian office.

The Soldiers at nights became pious, were clamorous about some kind of bucks, not particular whether green or yellow color. Oh! Christianity art thou Prostituted!

May 10, 1863

There has been fighting near Frederickburg, Virginia. The Federal army was repulsed and fell back in rather bad order. This took place about the fourth of this month.

Genl. Braggs army is lying at Tulahoma and at Shelbyville, said to be in good condition. The wounded with him reported to be nearly all well.

The Federal soldiers here are taking matters quite easy, lying about in the shade eating and drinking. There is quite a mania among them in the way of remodeling their camps. They haul large quantities of cedar brush to ornament their tents, make latice frame and work the branches in. This destroys a great deal of timber. It appears they came to destroy, it matter not which way.

On Easter day, they had quite a celebration among the Catholic portion of the army, Genl. Rosecrans being of that faith. They had several tents fitted for the purpose and highly ornamented with curtains and otherwise with such articles as they could borrow, flags and banners displayed, the Brass band was in requisition, had one or two Priests on the occaision. Mass was kept up for several days for the good of souls that was in and out of purgatory. The priests and some of the head men could pray through the day and at night drink liquor and carouse the balance of the time. These are a godly people.

Besides this nothing of much interest. Things appear to be quiet with the exception can hear of some skirmishing in different sections of the country with cavalry forces, nothing serious occurring from it at any time.

The armys on the Potomac threatning each other. We have a great many dispatched, more to keep up an excitement than any thing else among the soldiers.

But the greatest excitement here among the soldiers is buying ginger cakes, pyes and lemonade. May add whiskey, as the effects are seen some times by their being overcome by the article. When this happens, as a punishment, the guilty will have to carry a rail on his shoulder for about two hours each day for two or three days or a headless flour barrel, with the head of the man out at top, for this length of time. This is for getting drunk, a mode of punishment in the camps by the Yankees. They dont appear to mind it much. Some of them would be willing any time to carry rail or barrel, for a good swig of whiskey.

Some of the boys, as they call themselves, are troublesome, slipping round citizens gardens and stealing vegetables as they get of any size, onions in particular. They will go any length to obtain a fiew onions.

May 20, 1863

Two or three of the churches being now clear as hospitals. The Methodist denomination get up a petition to have public preaching, having a preacher in charge. They of course expected to have their own church for that purpose when the permit was granted. Not so. When they offered to take possession were disappointed by a man the name of —

H.A. Patterson

Who claimed to be a Methodist preacher from the South, 'a true abolitionist.' He takes charge and will not give up to the rightful owners. They of course, have to look out another place for their purpose, being on the side of the submissive.

And this man Patterson may be a christian, in this case did not appear to shew much brotherly love to persons evan of the same profession as himself, although Ivey will meet him with a hearty shake of the hand, how are you? brother Patterson!

Here he is! of moderate hight, stout built, black hair and heavy whiskers, broad face, dark skin, eyes no matter, short bull neck and may add bull headed, disposed to hear things his own way, opens church of Sundays for preaching, has for a short time moderate gatherings of soldiers, not over doz. women and about thirty men, hospital nurses. After a time appears to have fiew or no hearers, all going to the other meeting. On enquiring, reason is his own men have no confidence in him as a preacher or a man, is one of that class called chaplins to the army, but likely man in search of Green Backs than he is in search after the good of souls.

We see him associating with a Negro preacher who is familiar to us all by the name of Brack, a tall stout indolent thick blubber liped fellow. At this time feels on an equality with his colleague, likely is.

Well, these two chums may be seen sitting together in the Pulpit? Yes! Doling out hymns and prayers to the God forsaken. From the symptom, most likely shall have to notice these divinities several times in the course of notes.

Our Preacher, 'Mr. H.,' had to take the oath allegience before he would be allowed to officiate. Was considered a rebel to his God or the Yankees, possibly both. However, we look on him as a good christian man. He had large meetings every sabbath, citizens and Yankees, men, women and children. He preaches in the church generally denominated Campbellite or Christian. Has in connection a Sabbath School for children, well attended.

June 1, 1863

Still at a loss for any thing to note, with respect to the movement of the armys. From appearance the Federal army here are getting anxious to be doing something. Duty calls. They feel the necessity to rouse up. They have been lying in camp five months at the expense of Uncle Sam, living up his bounty with the aid of the rebel assistance, which has not been small in its share.

They have eat out this section of country. Orders are made for a move, the necessary quantity of rations for several days also ordered. Supposed on to the front. A division or so moves a fiew miles and settles down quietly. In this way, they continue for some time, acting somewhat hesitating.

All eyes are turned toward Vicksburg. Great demonstration now being made at that place. Heavy fighting going on. It is besieged on all sides, still holds out, will likely have to fall, the forces too great to subsist much longer.

The weather at this time is dry, dusty and warm. At ordinary times would be complaining of the great suffering of crops, for the want of rain. Crops is a thing that can trouble us little in this part of country, so on that score will rest contented.

This is the season we usually have our big June meeting at Old Providence Church near Pierce Mill. Instead of the hundred vehickles crouded with joyous crouds, dressed in their best, dashing along the road, venting a hearty laugh and causing the dust to rise like clouds at the setting of the sun of a summer evening - instead —

We have long lines of dusty cavalrymen with sabers clanking at their sides, navy pistols batted round them, their countenances covered with long hair and whiskers pitching along at a furious rate, horses hoofs roaring like distant thunder.

June 24, 1863

The siege at Vicksburg continues. The Federal are determined to take the place this time, if possible. Have been shelling the place for some days, without effecting much. The losses heavy on their side, in killed and wounded.

Frequent raids and skirmishing going on over the country with the cavalry. There is fighting in Virginia, some losses on both sides, but no battle of importance.

Genl. Rosecrans Moves Front

To day Gen. Rosecrans makes a move to the front with the whole army. The weather has been very dry for some time. By the time they are all on the road, it commences raining, continues all day. The army is divided in these parts, one on the Shelbyville pike, one on Manchester pike, the third on the Readyville. In this way they advance. By the time they get ten miles off, heavy skirmishing commenced. At some of the points considerable difficulty in beating back the Confederates, they having all the advantages of hills and good positions, and generally a better acquaintance of the country. Some of the federal regiments suffered greatly from losses, the Confederate but slightly. On all the routs, the ground was strongly contested, the Confederate fighting and falling back. Slowly. They were several days getting to Shelbyville. It was thought there would have been some hard fighting at this place, but such was not the case, as Gen. Bragg continued to fall back to Tulahoma.

When Genl. Rosecrans moved from Murfreesboro, he scarcely left forces sufficient to man the fortification. Those that were left were afraid they would be "gobbled" up, would frequently speak about rebel cavalry raids and would make threats. If such should be the case, they had orders to shell the town and burn it up. This was supposed to make the citizens afraid too.

That sort of talk did not intimidate the citizens in the least. They had became quite indifferent as to what they might do, in the way of shelling. The town could not be much worsted unless it was to knock down the balance of houses.

To shew the least of it then, was not much bravery displayed by those "Veteran troops," who were hid behind breastworks with their cannon pointed on a fiew old men, women and children, threatening them. If they let the rebel cavalry come on us, we will shoot, as though the defenseless citizens could help the coming of cavalry to town if they wished. This might scare at first, not now, Gen. Vancleave.

July 4, 1863

We have a small demonstration of independance day. Thirty four guns were discharged for the states, all in - so far as shooting.

July 7, 1863

Have had continued rain more or less for the last fifteen days, which has made the roads in some parts almost impassable for wagon, trains or soldiers marching. Numbers of wagons broke down on the way. The artillery had great difficulty in making way, but with all the difficulties, the Federal army finally arrive at Shelbyville, being fatigued and nearly woarn out, and of course fiewer men than it started with.

Gen. Lee makes an advance into Pennsylvania with his army. A very severe battle takes place at Gettysburg, the losses being quite heavy on both sides. He gains his object and falls back to his former position.

Gen. Mead is on his own side of the Rapidan with a hankering "on to Richmond" from some cause, feels more safe to remain where he is.

The Telegraph men are greatly exercised to keep up the news. The times a little dull in their business, but they have to fournish the associated press with a certain amount of matter, so as to keep up an excitement with the paper dealers and readers.

They have Mead one day crossing the Rapidan, and in day or so, he is back safe. Lee has disappeared with his army, not known where he has gone, in a fiew days turns up about where he was. This is about the movement of the armys in Virginia.

July 15, 1863

Things about Murfreesboro generally quiet. The citizens feel much relieved since the move of the Federal army from this place, begin to breath a little more easy, although are surrounded with pickets and pass papers, Negros and dogs, to our hearts content. The Negros are imigrating more regular to the promised land, some days by the wagon load, with their baggage, old camp kettles, Blankets, quilts, and with what finery the women have managed to steal from mistress before they leave, to make a display when in town. All have a disposition to straitten their wool. It has to undergo a training, in strings.

Negro Idea of Pleasure

One in the country, hears how they are getting on in town, concludes to come and see. He comes in, visits among his acquaintance, which may be found from ten to fifty in a house, of all sizes and ages. Windows stoped with old blue pants and coats to keep the wind out. Every thing else, about in proportion.

He tells his friends his business and complaining says he has to be up by day, cut wood, make fires and draw water, all that sort of thing. He is tired of it. They tell him, in town he can sleep to eight oclock in the morning, get up when he please. When he is sleepy lie down again and do nothing, no trouble. Is satisfied "I is guine to come in right straits. is tired of work, bless the lord! Such is their idea of comfort. Have no thought of much else.

July 20, 1863

At this date have Rosecrans at Shelbyville, Bragg at Tulahoma, Lee on one side of the Rapidan, Mead on the other, suppose in a safe place. The other army much as they were, all now rubbing their guns and mending other difficulties. Are in hot pursuit of Morgan in Indiana, say they will have him this time, if he dont get away. Forrest in West Ten., tis said playing smash with peoples property, such as stealing horses and robbing generally (the Yankees never do such thing). Wheeler is about, looking for an easy place to pull up the R. Road, throw off the cars and catch some unsuspecting Yankee in the ruin. Telegraph man busy in gitting up bogus dispatches for the editors. Here I scarcly able to get a single item to note.

July 25, 1863

Move up dates a little. Nothing of importance transpired since last date, when we left the armys reposing, putting their war implements in order.

Morgan, from the latest accounts, has got over into Indiana with a heavy force of cavalry, for what purpose not able to find out. The people of that part of country have raised forces and are in hot persuit of him. He has done no particular damage to any thing or person as yet.

The siege of Vicksburg is still going on, great efforts are made to reduce the place, also that of Port Hudson. Not much accomplished yet.

The weather at this time is quite warm and dry, becoming very dusty here.

August 1, 1863

Vicksburg has finally fallen and Port Hudson. The losses to the Federal army was great in storming and taking the place. The losses to the Confederate was not very great in killed and wounded, but the whole garrison surrendered and gave up the place. This caused a damper to the Confederate cause, by this a large portion of their supplies were cut off from their army.

An attact on Charleston was made about the same time with less success to the Federal army. Heavy bombarding was had for several days. When they finally withdraw their vessels of war, badly worsted by the engagement, they took some unimportant point, which they have undertaken to fortify.

The movements in Virginia not of much importance, each army watching for advantage of the other. The Telegraph men are keeping up the greatest excitement of the armys in that quarter of the country. According to their accounts, movements going on every day of the greatest importance.

The Federal army occupy Shelbyville, Ten. at this time. The Confederate having evacuated and fallen back to Chatanooga, where it is supposed they will fortify their position, being a strong place to hold with moderate force.

August 10, 1863

Genl. Rosecrans about this date, is making a move in the direction of Manchester. Things quite easy about Murfreesboro, the Fed. army having been reduced at this place, giving the appearance of dulness. Little business doing by any person, a fiew trying to get up a small trade on apples and potatoes, eggs and such small articles as they can collect.

The Smoking and Whitling croud are having meetings every day, speculating on what may happen. All will generally have some startling news to relate, what he has heard or understood had happened.

At these meetings every thing relating to the armys would have the appearance of being well planned, how they would most likely operate and the general results.

Thus the days are filled up. At the close, each member wends his way home, satisfied he understand how matters are, for it looks to him, as clear as mud.

Officer or Union League

At the time the Federal army were here, the officers and their preachers formed a society at one of the churches for conference, or planning some business, which was called an officers meeting. This was kept up some time and finally resolved itself into what was called by them, a Union League, or enquiring meeting. At this they would make speeches and relate what they had seen and heard during the week, and would generally give "Sesesh" a pretty severe basting in their harangues. Any of the members were at liberty of speaking and would be called on to make some remarks for the edification of the meeting.

Just here will introduce one of the prominent members of this meeting —

Revd. W---r

It is costomary for the army to have chaplain attached to it, as a safe guard to the morals of the soldiers. In the course of events, this Mr. W. offers his servises to the Confederate army as Chaplain, Being of course pious, disposed and very strong "Sesesh" proclivities and the rights of the south greatly at heart, was elected to the office of Chaplain to the army. Being a poor young man, had not the means to purchase a horse (being necessary to have one), a paper sent round, the amount raised necessary, a horse is purchased for him. In the mean time, he courted and married (a short time before the retreat of Bragg), to a young Lady of the strongest rebel feelings in the neighborhood. This of course made him all right on that subject.

Now this young man was studying Theology at the Baptist University, (this Baptist church furnish chaplains as well as others)— NB. The devil has made arrangements with all denominations for chaplains as his confederates, to carry out his devilish plans, seems to have preference for that class of individuals.

He, not being thorough in his studies, thought he could fill the bill, so on Gen. Braggs retreat, he follows. This is the last we hear from him for some time.

His home is in Lincoln county. Late, in the spring, his wife gets through the Yankee lines to him. Dont say he deserted his past. He was caught, the oath of allegience was pored down him, is now a "loyal" man to all intents. The next we see these two specimens of "Sesesh" returning to Murfreesboro, as tame as a pair of kittens out of a rain. This is one side of picture.

He is here now comfortably located, out of much danger. As he had been so strong on one side, it became necessary to shew his devotion to the other, to make a balance of affairs.

In passing about, he is invited by the "Union League" to call in, and take a hand with them. He accepts. The first night, goes into the middle of the meeting and makes a full hand. In the course of the evening is called on to make a talk. Of course, pretended to shew a little modesty on the occaision, but finally let out in a lengthy harangue. He gave "Sesesh" particular thunder, told of all their doings, none of them good, how they would treat the prisoners and what he tought ought to be done with them. Declares himself a Union man, was for the old "Stars and Stripes" all the time. Tells of what he heard in the streets of some sympathiser (possibly one who had helped to pay for his horse), what he thought ought to be done with such persons, applause. Now, of course, a good member, down on all rebels and sympathisers.

Is now doing a good business in the picture way in this city. May be well to stick a pin here.

Subsequently after his arrival, his father makes his appearance as a refugee. Had some awful tales to relate to his son, of bad treatment by the rebels, although within the Yankee boundary. Complained of bush whackers, destroying his property, and were after him all the time, to kill him. Son become very indignant, turns pale, declares he will have revenge. He will raise a cavalry company, go right off there, scour the country, whip them out. Knows them. They are a sett of thieving rascals.

From the general appearance one would conclude he would lead a different direction to where the enemy. This is an outline of the Revd. W-, the sketch may do to know him by.

While on this subject, cant help introducing another type, in the shape of chaplain. Before we proceed further, may be necessary to offer an apology.

It will be understood that it is not the wish to pry more hard on the class of persons than they deserve. There are exceptions in all cases admitted. There are men in the capacity of Chaplains that are christians, do their whole duty, but they are like angels visits.

August 15, 1863

But little change in things round about this section of country. All move on as well as might be expected under the circumstances.

Morgan and a portion of his command has been captured in Ohio, part escaped. Report say when they were found, they were hotly persuied, that they divided off in small companies for the purpose of escape. By this means many made good their retreat. He and several of his officers are in prison at Columbus, Ohio.

Sept. 12, 1863

Up to this date very little transpiring of any thing worthy of note. Preparation is making and from all appearance, there will be some work soon, but at what point uncertain.

Genl. Rosecrans is making a move on toward Chatanooga. He has nearly all his forces with him, and tis thought will make an attact on that place.

Sept. 15, 1863

Genl. Bragg has received large reinforcement by Genl. Longstreet from Virginia, and fallen back to Chicamauga creek with his army.

Sept. 20, 1863

Genl. Rosecrans has been following after Bragg for some days past, for the purpose of making an attact.

To day an attact was made on Gen. Bragg at Chicamauga Creek. The ground is low, flat, level place, thick set with small undergroth, about fifteen miles from Chatanooga, at some places a man could be seen but a short distance. The Confederate were rather ambushed in consequence of the groth. Artillery could be of little use, as it was impossible to get sights. The fighting had to be done with musketry. The first day battle was hard contested, continued on till dark. The Confederate kept the ground during the night. The losses was heavy on both sides, it being an open field fight. There could not be much difference as to loss on either side.

Early the next day, the battle was renewed and lasted the greater part of the day. Finally the Federal lines gave way and some of the regiments, in confusion, fled to Chatanooga. They all made good their retreat to that place.

It is said had it not have been for Gen. Thomas coming up in time, most likely Rosecrans army would have been captured, or at least the greater portion taken prisoners. Large numbers were taken, wounded and dead attended as usual.

It was the intention of Gen. Bragg to make the second days attact at about day light, and so ordered. Gen. Polk did not obey orders, in this case, that were given him. By this neglect the enemy had more time to reinforce, which they did. His object in getting so far off from Chatanooga to fight the battle was he felt satisfied with the forces he then had, that when the enemy were on a retreat, they would become demoralized by being hard pressed and make for the river to cross and in crossing would capture before they would get out of reach.

When the battle was fought, it is said, the bushes was cut down by the bullets. Looks strange, how a man could escape being struck.

Gen. Rosecrans army, having been so much reduced by the Chicamauga battle, that it became necessary that he should have reinforcements, and so orders from Virginia.

Oct. 1, 1863

Genl. Wheeler, with his cavalry, (having been in the neighborhood of Chatanooga for the purpose of making a raid and tearing up the R. Road and foraging through the country), strikes out in the direction of McMinnville, Ten. A day or so after a force of Federal cavalry under Wilder, in pursuit. From appearance they are not over anxious to come up with Wheeler. It is understood they made convenient to be a day or so behind all the way.

Wheeler arrives at McMinnville, makes an attact on the place, captures what forces that is there and paroles them (report say nine hundred), did no damage to the place. He now turns his course in the direction of Murfreesboro, passed through Woodbury traveling slow in this direction. On this part of the road, Wilder had liked to have come up with him, finding the difficulty he was getting into, makes a "strategetic" move to the right as though he was going another direction. This was supposed to evade a fight with Wheeler.

Wheeler advances within three miles of Murfreesboro, then turns to the left of the Town in direction where the R. Road crosses Stones River to a bridge. At this place he captures the guard that were stationed there. They made some resistance. The bridge was burned, the rail road for some distance tore up. He made some delay here, to give his waggon train an opportunity to make their way to Shelbyville.

Wheeler had no intention of coming to this place, being too well informed how things were situated, in point of fortification works. To have made any attempt would have been time spent and probably a considerable loss of life and property to the citizens. After delaying as long as he wished at the crossing of the river, moved in the direction of Shelbyville.

In the evening of the same day (Monday), Coln. Wilder with his cavalry force make their appearance on the Woodbury pike east of town, and about night they enter the place. Things looked a little blue. No one scarcely knew what would be the result of the matter. Soldiers that were about town appeared to be greatly alarmed. Now and then could see two or three start off to the fortification in a run after taking first a look back and saw cavalry comeing. "Sure it was the Sesesh" there would be small crouds of citizens and soldiers standing about. In one of these crouds some person fired a pistol from a distance (this small gathering was at the door of Jos. Nelson on Main Street). The ball struck a small child of his on the side of the face, but fortunately did not kill. Some of the soldiers were disposed to think or say the shot was done by a citizen at one of their men which was on horse back. No particular inquiry was made about the matter. No doubt but it was done by some foul hearted Yankee from settler house of course.

This all happened just about the time Wilders cavalry were coming in sight.

The next morning the cavalrymen were making a great shew of hurry to persue Wheeler. They did not get on the road until late in the day and many did not leave the town until late in the evening. In fact, none of them went far out until they had learned that Wheeler had left the neighborhood.

October 4, 1863

Taking a view of things about Murfreesboro, find matters not in so pleasant situation as could be wished. The Federal forces at this place was weak, all had been taken front that could be well spared, which left barely enough to man the forts and keep up the provost guard, so they felt a little ticklish as to their chances of holding things in the right place. The report of Wheelers cavalry was enormous. They thought four or five to one of them, and as they would likely come in different directions to make the attact, it would give them their hands full to keep them off.

The Alarm

The alarm commenced after supper on Sunday night, among citizens and others. Orders are issued by officers for all to move their valuables to the fortification. Things began to go in confusion, wagons and all hands that could be got, was immediately put to work packing and hauling all the goods that were in the stores, running all night. By morning the stores were clear of every thing but shelves.

They would haul the goods, or whatever it might be, throw them down in piles, with the promise of having them guarded. Those that felt queamish about danger would stay there.

As for the safety of goods, it looked as reasonable to put them out in open field for safe keeping, it was nothing more. As being out of danger, this was not the place for that. The woods would have been preferable. Well, here we find goods and timid men lying in piles for safe keeping from "Sesesh."

As for the negros, it looked as might be the day of judgement with them. They were seen going to and fro with their estates on their heads and in their hands, trying to get admission within the fortification grounds. Some did not know what to do, asking some one to protect them, say "I belongs to you!" All now as gentle as lambs, who would have been impudent to you the day before.

We have got all of the timid or those who think the union sentiment would be a verry great objection to their safety, placed in the hands of the rebels. Many of these that class themselves here would scarcely be noticed by either side of the question.

There you see piles of boxes. Here and there with the owners watching, feeling anxious about which might be taken first, their goods or that of their neighbors, or themselves first.

The negros they too have some checks of conscious as to what would likely be their fate if the 'rebs' should catch them. Thus they are seen.

Last, not least, the fortification men, how are they? Every man had his station, are within, doors closed, their guns pointed at some object, court house or some certain dwelling in town. Determined to shell the place as they say, if the rebels come in, burn it up. Orders to that effect said to be issued by the commander, to shell and destroy the property of all.

Note — This may be a wise order. At first glance, it looks silly. How could the citizens help any cavalry coming that wished, they not being armed and not their place to have arms. It is soldiers employment.

At one time they at the fortifications came very near letting loose their war dogs on Col. Wilders cavalry as they were making their appearance in the Eastern part of town. Thought it was Gen. Wheeler. The excitement was intense for some time. It gradually died off as it was understood he was moving off in the direction of Shelbyville. This is the way matters were on Monday.

This day, the day after the rebel cavalry was in the neighborhood, permission given to return. Every thing was on the move again to town, business, appearance, stores fixing up, commissary wagons on the move bringing in their provisions. Many a dollars worth was lost or stolen. Scarcely a person who moved out but could say he had lost some in the transaction. Such is the fate of war.

Genl. Wheeler arrived at Shelbyville Oct. 6th, his wagon train also. His men were not particular to have a formal introduction. They introduced themselves in some what rough manner, and in a short time have every thing in confusion. They go to stores and help themselves to whatever came in the way, goods, shoes and groceries, without respect to persons or prices, or what they thought of it.

Broke open safes, took what money they could find, loaded their wagons and started them on. The soldiers took a great many articles they had no use for. They did not molest the citizens, more than take their property, though there was a good many that had considerable fears as to their safety. They were professed to be Union Men. This place and county thought to be the strongest inclined that way. However they got off without hurt, more than loss of property. It was bad enough.

Wheeler and his cavalry remain about this place until the trains have time to get some distance, then start. Their course is in the direction of the shoals on Tennessee river, for the purpose of crossing there, which they did.

Col. Wilder Following

On Tuesday, the next day after the Fed. Cavalry arrived in Murfreesboro, about twelve oclock, Col. Wilder starts off, seemingly in great haste, in pursuit of Wheeler who is now at Shelbyville. He arrives at the edge of the town and camps for the night, Wheeler and his men on the other side, but by the time Wilder saw proper to move against the other, he had gone many miles on his way and continued unmolested till he gets to the Ten. River. He crossed all his wagons safely, and before he could get all his men over, Wilder comes up just in time to capture a fiew of the rear guard and horses. He now returns, with the fiew prisoners has caught.

Note — This is about the substance of the raid, round from near Chattanooga by Wheeler, and Coln. Wilder, at a respectful distance from him all the way. Did not understand which had the largest force. Report says Wheeler had not been over the river long before he recrossed and is again at large in the country. It is said he destroyed a good deal army stores at McMinnville when passed there.

October 7th, 1863

Things is now settling down and have a quiet appearance. All have now got their goods and other matters regulated. Business has the appearance of going on as usual. The people from the country now begin to come in to trade with their produce, make small purchases and return home after going through the pass process.

Confiscators

About this time a man came here from Nashville, his name dont recollect, but he called himself a confiscating agent. Dont know whether he is a preacher or not, presume he is, from his appearance. Had a sanctified look but otherwise a pest man in his manner, on the Yankee style. He puts up with a Mr. Patterson (previously noticed). His business, so he says, is to collect all the abandoned property of the citizens who have gone south. Did not learn where he got his license or whether he had any, presume he had not. Now to come at the matter right and in plain English, his business was nothing more nor less than stealing. The citizens had by this time become so submissive that they could not object much to any thing - even worse.

This man remains but a day or two in the town, appoints Patterson as his agent to act, returns to Nashville or some where else. Is seen no more.

This man Patterson, having been here about nine months, had been mixing and preaching among the negros during the time. Had become well posted as to who was gone and whether they had left any thing and where at, the name of the articles. This he learns from the negros, as they generally helped their master to move the articles and always with the Yankees truthful people. Thus equiped with the necessary information, starts. All he has to do is to procure a small wagon, go to Mr. A.B. C.s houses and call for articles in the name of the Government. If a denial of any thing he produced the memorandum. Of course, Mr. A. has to acknowledge such things are there. They deliberately take possession and load the wagon, such as house hold furniture, all sorts Librarys, pictures, etc., carry them to a store room for such things. At this part of the process the two friends are acting in connection. The articles being pretty well collected up, confiscator disappears and his friend Petterson is published as acting as agent for him.

As Patterson can hear of a new case Rob is punctual to do so. In one or two cases the persons would not shell out. This did not appear to molest, droped it, went to some other than could be worked on. These things are deposited in Jos. Nelsons drug store room.

Having made a slight street acquaintance with Mr. Patterson, one day seeing the door open and soldiers carrying off three or four books each, curiosity prompted to go there, see what was going on, likely pick up an item, knowing his business.

Ah! Mr. Patterson! Opening drug store? You sure to have a good many things on hand. No! Am only collecting up my jewels. Come in. Walk in, look round the room. Here is Bureaus with papers and old letters and other small articles in drawers, Bead steads, all kinds, wash stands and some articles belonging, window hangings, boxes of various family articles in them. Family Portraits, Large Pier glasses and smaller. Boxes of Books and other things of the kind, and some boxes of Law Books. Of these he has the lids off, airing them, as he says, and a hundred other things on hand. The missclaneous books he is distributing to the soldiers to read. These, he says, would be of little value to the government — But — The Law Books will bring something, as they are valuable.

How are you going to dispose, or when will they be sold? Well! Suit will be brought. They will be condemned, will be either sold here or at Nashville.

Looking over law books. See Mr. Ransoms name. I know that man! Yes! Suppose he is in the rebel army. No, he is dead. Well! Will never do him any good. There is Mr. Burtons Books and there is Palmers. These are clever men. I suppose they are in the sesesh army. They ought to load every thing. So it goes, with the books.

See some portraits. As you are an old citizen, I suppose you may know them, recognise an acquaintance and friend, insist on having that one. He, I reckon, is in the rebel army. No, he has been dead more than fifteen years.. Indirectly refuse.

Gives a slight history of himself. I once practiced Law, quit a business of twenty five hundred dollars and took to the Pulpit. Had a law library, worth fifteen hundred dollars, which I sold, have since wished had kept it. Thought here is a chance to replenish for nothing. No doubt he is.

In a short time call again. Look round. No Law Books. Furniture disappeared, scarcely any thing of much value to be seen in the room. Question! Where is it gone? Possibly the friend who was with him now at Nashville or some other point might answer the question. The government!!

Romans 2 chap. 21 verse - Patterson

He is now quite a business man. See him passing in all directions over town. Occupies a house, large enough for a Country Hotel, all to himself. Allows no one to occupy with him. If some of his kind come along, wish to get a room, refers to some place that is crouded for room. It is thought the house he holds, which belongs to an estate, he is disposed to appropriate to his own use and benefit.

To hear him talk, one would think he was the most patriotic. Talks largely of the doings of our army, and what they may do.

At one time there was a talk of wanting the house he is in for hospital purposes. Would have to look for other quarters. At this gets very much out of sorts, made heavy complaint, thought it was hard for him to be turned out of his house when there was Mr. R. and Mrs. B. and others who were citizens, living comfortably. Nothing said to them about wanting houses. He did't like it at all.

A Soldiers Opinion of Him

Having made the acquaintance of an inteligent soldier from his part of country. In course of conversation, put the question, are you acquainted with preacher Patterson? Yes! Pretty well. How does he stand at home? Says he was a lawyer and now see him in the army as chaplain. Relates - At home, what I would call a jack-leg lawyer, attended county or justice courts, got a dollar or two for pleading a case, or any such job as that did't get much to do either. Not looked on as much of a man. He took to preaching, got appointed to the place of chaplain of the army, came out with it. Soldiers look on him as a d-d hum-bug, have no confidence in him as a preacher. In fact, preachers are a nuisance to any army, generally get bad as the soldiers. If I was commander, not one should be allowed to come in camp.

Told him of articles he had collected as a confiscating officer. He is stealing. The government will never get a cent of the proceeds. I venture, if you would go to his house, at home, you would find hundreds of articles he had shipped there.

Thought as the soldier, a reasonable conjecture. He appeared to be honest in his statement. Querry: How many such cases are there over the country, stealing articles and sending home as trophies of war and for profit, as the Yankees always have that in view in almost every case. Now leave him for the present. He is on hand. Will keep an eye on him.

October 12, 1863

Now, advance dates. Matters have settled down quietly. Hear of no raids, nor much news of any kind.

Genl. Rosecrans is now receiving large reinforcements from Virginia, going on to Chatanooga, as he holds that place, and fortifying his position. A large number has been added to the forces at this place. They now feel more comfortably situated in points of strength, in case of a raid being made on the place.

Business is beginning to improve. New business houses are being established, goods getting quite plenty, groceries also, all at high prices to what we have been used formerly. Thus earlier 40 to 60 cts domestic, from 50 to 70 other, cotton goods in proportion. Sugar 30 to 35, Coffee 40 to 50 and so, articles in this line.

We have what is called a board trade, that is, a man who grants permits to merchants to purchase goods for a trade store.

The county is allowed sixty thousand dollars per month. No merchant is to have over three thousand permitted to purchase goods, from that down. It is not all that wish to do business can get a chance.

Process of selling — Costomer wish to purchase, he must first get a permit of board trade, name the articles, makes purchase, merchant to make out a bill and duplicate and keep a memorandum himself on book. This bill to be approved by the board, if over five dollars to pay from five to twenty five cents for approving. Pro Vost also approve. These bills of purchase is pasted to a paper which has an oath printed which costomer has to sign, a copy kept. This is all done to keep any goods from going through the lines South.

Merchant has to give a bond with two good securities for double the amount of permit granted him. His permit to be approved every month if he make purchase.

A short time since, the seller of any thing had to ask costomer if he had taken the oath or was loyal. If not, could get nothing until that was done. If merchant sold without oath having been taken by costomer, he was liable to have his house shut up and business stoped.

The Provost is quite busy every day, administering the oath, or "galvanizing." Some of them are particular to have the thing well done. They make the applicant repeat the words after them, then sign bonds for some certain amount security, one as a passport, the other is filed away.

With all this trouble business appeared to be quite good. Some of the business houses took in cash, some days as much as eight hundred dollars and from that down, according to their business. It took a good deal money to get a small lot goods. Salt sold as high as twenty eight dollars per barrel. As it became plenty the price came down.

Produce from the country was more plenty than was reasonable to suppose under circumstances, as it looked like the country had been foraged to death. Beef Market plentiful at eight cents, pork about the same. Chickens twenty five cents, butter 25, eggs 20. Every thing in this way appeared to be plentiful, though it may have been the force of market to raise green backs to make other purchases in stores. No other money would do any good. Every thing sells and fast.

Occaisionally see wagons loaded with cotton on the way to Nashville, the price ranging at sixty five cents per pound - moderate!

One thing is abolished, and tis hoped forever, is the credit system. No such thing is known at this time. All cash. Every man now for himself, no faith in his neighbors punctuality. Pay as you go. The system can be made to work well. If kept up we shall have but little use for sheriffs and constables and justices, trying men for debt, which is one of the greatest perplexities of the country.

The note shavers business, with the cash system, will die out, which is another draw back in a community. Shaving has encouraged too many drones to be humming about, living on the labor of the weary and causing a blight on the improvement of the county.

October 18, 1863

Up to this time have had but little use for hospitals. Not more than one in use for the sick of the camps. All others had been cleared out. But now, a new call for hospitals is being made, for sick and wounded from Chatanooga. Business houses or stores having been established in the rooms that had been previously used for hospitals, these stores had to move and find other places for business. Hotel building was taken for hospital use. A large number of bunks being made, and other necessary articles for that use collected.

It is supposed another battle will come off shortly about Chatanooga. The wounded that was there was sent forward to this place and Nashville. Quite a call for negros to wait on hospitals, washing, getting wood and other servises. This class of servises could be well spared, as there is a large number walking about doing nothing for themselves or any one else. They are enjoying freedom.

Oct. 25, 1863

Genl. Rosecrans is superceeded. He is ordered to head quarters, to report some slight charge being brought against him by some of the officers, so report say. But we are of the impression it was because he let Genl. Bragg drive him back from Chicamauga Creek in the late battle there.

Genl. Thomas takes the place of Rosecrans. Things will take a new feature. There are a good many troops leaving here for the front. At this time a good deal rain. The roads in bad order for moving troops.

Hear of but little fighting in any direction. Now and then a little skirmishing with the cavalry forces. Nothing serious at any time. The army in Virginia doing little or nothing. No important news from Charleston. One place appears hard to take, being well fortified on every point. The news papers at a loss for something startling to make papers sell.

Lincoln is calling for three hundred thousand more troops for his army. Is creating quite an excitement in the Northern part of the country, to know who will have to turn out. The talk is, they will have to raise them by draft. A trial will be first made for volunteering. Large amounts of money subscribed to pay bountys to volunteers and buy substitutes.

The better class prefer staying at home, but are willing to help to carry the war on. They are for crushing out the rebellion. The fact is, are more for crushing out the negro system, laboring more to carry that point than any other good. Scarcely ever say any thing about the old Stars and Stripes they used to worship so much in times past. Negro is the theme, the down trodden race who they say, ought to be free and independant. In the next breath, say they shall not cross the Ohio river. When that idea is advanced for them to go, these are willing to dam them.

The officers are using great exertion to get the old veterans, as the soldiers are now called, to reinlist again, are offering to give thirty days furlough to go home before their time expires and extra bounties. This takes quite well for the majority. If they go out have nothing to do but follow their old business of loafing about the streets of cities. Many of the officers in the same fix as they are. In the army getting from one to two hundred dollars a month. Of course, makes them feel quite patriotic to fight the rebellion. They prefer it should continue than stop.

They are all generally living better when in the army than they do at home.

There are many of the soldiers rejoin the army against there better feelings, by force of circumstance, that is, when a large number of his comrades step forward, they do so too, to keep from being jeered, or called cowardly, or something else. No doubt that a large number, who in times past said if they thought they were fighting for the freedom of the negro would lay down their gun tomorrow, are enrolled for another three years services, notwithstanding they now see they are fighting for the negro and nothing else. Mens ways are strange, not to be accounted for.

The First Negro Soldiers

The latter part of last summer, the first Negro Military Company was raised here. It was commanded and drilled by the redoubtable Captain O.C. Rounds of the "under the bed" notoriety, a man who is qualified for that office - how fallen! Once could command a community of soldiers, and citizens were at his beck and call. His words was the law. Could put in or take out of prison when he pleased. Now, Wham!! A captain over a lot of wooly headed, blubber lipped, bandy shanked, tray footed negros!! A deserving compliment indeed!

A short time after a fiew more companys was added. They now take the name of regiment and is commanded by a little red hair'd and red whisker'd dutchman, who could not speak English very plain. They drilled round about here a week or so and all disappeared, to what point the Devil only knows - Rounds and all.

It seems the Coln. wished to make a display of himself and his men of "Colour," so while going out on dress parade, as it is called, makes convenient on his way to pass through town, passing through as many streets as his rout would admit of. His object he best knew himself, but it looked more like a taunt or insult than any thing else to the citizens. It did make the blood boil.

The post commanders good sense, understanding the nature of the thing, seeing no good to be derived from such exibition, ordered the gallant Coln. to make no more exibits with his regiment within the town limits.

These gallants were all draped in the usual sky blue Yankee cloths, all clean and new cloth, round top caps, shoes and to finish dress, all had on their hands white gloves. When the officers, white coloured men, carrying their swords bare hand. Ebony had learned to march quite well, keep the step and when their backs were turned to you had much the appearance of a Yankee Soldier. They are now gone. May the devil be with them.

Surprising Gen. Bragg

Gen. Bragg, after the retreat of Gen. Rosecrans to Chatanooga, follows, gets in possession of Look Out Mountain and mission ridge, a strong position to hold. He was in a situation that he could look in the camps of the Federal, but too far off to have much effect with his cannon, being from two to four miles. He annoyed them by not letting boats pass to Chatanooga. The two armys were in this position for some weeks. Neither could damage the other much, although shots were frequently exchanged. The Federal army were reduced to short rations. They were in a situation that some thing had to be done, spedily, or be compelled to fall back to better quarters. Finally an attempt was made to storm Bragg in his position, which was a perilous one. They however, "distributed" their forces, which was to make attacts at different points of the mountain. All things ready, they make the move.

Gen. Bragg was taken by surprise. The morning of the attact, there was a heavy fogg on the top of the mountain, extending about half way down the sides. They could not see the enemy until they had nearly gained their point.

At this time the battle commenced furiously, on both sides. The federal had gained several good positions before there was any chance to repulse them. The fighting was kept up vigerously on both sides, the Confederate giving way slowly.

The attact at Mission Ridge was about the same time. The losses were heavy on both sides of killed and wounded. The Confederate lost a large number of prisoners, being cut off by flank movements. They retreated in good order. The Federal held the ground, having also lost many prisoners.

Had Gen. Bragg not been surprised in consequence of the dense fog which was on the mountain, it would have been almost impossible to take the place, as a portion is appearantly perpendicular. Ordinarily a place like this, with a small force, could keep a very large one at bay.

It is said a great many of Braggs men are daly deserting him. Almost every day prisoners are seen passing here captured, and many deserters. This class came in and are made "all right."

November 1, 1863

The Federal army send their stores to Bridgeport by R. Road, then wagon to Chatanooga, a distance over thirty miles, which proved to be difficult in consequence of roads being almost impassable with deep mud. Now are sending by boat to that place. Some of the soldiers told they were reduced to about fourth rations at one time, while Bragg was holding the mountain.

An order has been issued in consequence of a raid on the R. Road in the neighborhood of Tullahoma. That the houses for five miles on each side of the road be burned or destroyed, if such thing happen again. This is hard on citizens. They have no power to keep off any cavalry that see proper to tear up the road.

While on this subject, a similar order was made at Murfreesboro a day or two after Wheeler came through the neighborhood with his cavalry.

The Pro. Vo. Marshall had ten of the most prominent citizens arrested and held as hostages for the doings of Confed. Cavalry. These men (a part), who have been under bond already for more than a year. Now their property will have to suffer and likely themselves in case of a raid on the R.R., the distance not specified how far they are bound to protect. They are scarcely allowed to go out of town with a permit.

There is neither sense nor justice in such order, is a stretch of power which would never be used by any who had a spark of manliness in his composition. Has a tendency to get up a supreme hatred for all such petty tyrants. Such are these hirelings.

Negro School

A school is now about to be established in Murfreesboro for the education of "coloured" persons, as the Yankees call them. Our model Mr. Patterson and his associate Brack take the matter in hand. Both pious men? They have a large meeting on Sunday evening, addresses delivered by each of the colaboures. Mr. Patterson gives the audience to understand they are equal to the white people and as capable to receive an education as they. Now was the time to begin while they had an opportunity. They should embrace it. Makes a pathetic appeal to their feelings, was eloquent on the occaision. After detaining them some time, sat down.

Mr. Brack now rises, with all the dignity of a Congo King, makes a fiew flourishes, sets out by giving very logical reasons for the necessity of getting an education, giving his own experience in the matter, how he had to steal the time from his masters work to get what little education he had, urged them to accept of the opportunity, not to delay, for you may never have such a chance again. He detains the hearers in this manner for a short time, then takes his seat. Appearantly satisfied with his effort on the occaision.

Patterson now rises, makes a proposition to get this school in operation (states it is to be a free school), that each member present will subscribe or throw in what can spare, to make a start. Every one can give something to this cause. Dont be backward. Bro. James will take the hat round and receive what you have to throw in. Here is quite a commotion among the members of the meeting to see who should get their dimes in the Bros hat first. The result of the collection, when counted out, was about one hundred and twenty dols. Thought this a good start to buy wood, etc.

A school will now be organized, that on Mondays we want you all to assemble in the basement of the Methodist church and provide yourself with a spelling book or primmer. You never had such time before. Want all to embrace the opportunity.

An Extract

Extract of Parson Brack James speech which was delivered on the inauguration of the free School of "Persons of Color."

My friends, this is a glorious time. You are all now as free as the water that goes down the river. You are no more under the thumb and fingers of your masters and mistresses. You are as free as they are. They cant lie in bed to be waited on by you, having you cutting wood and drawing water for them. They will have to do it themselves.

These Yankees, as we call them, are our friends. They have made a great light to shine on us, a glorious light. They are turning our gin houses into school houses, our cotton patches into gardens. They are going to give us an education. We are now as good as the white man.

I want you all to have an education, all to go to school, but I dont want any under sixteen years old to come yet a while. There is time enough for the young ones, after a while, as they are all free and can get schooling any time. The old ones needs it now. You must all come, never mind if your cloths are not so good. You must come. Put on the best you have. Dont loose the opportunity.

And the young ones too, must all get an education and when you get large enough to shoulder your gun, you can then fight for the country. You have a great and free country to fight for. You will have no more masters and mistresses to order you about when they please.

These Yankees, as we call them, are our friends. They have give us freedom. They are not the bad people we are told they were. They have cast our bonds and chains from us. They love the black people. They are fighting for us and we ought to fight for them. So the little boys must come to school and learn their books. When they get large enough, they can then be soldiers and go out and fight for our glorious country."

Mr. Patterson made concluding remarks, was much in the same strain, not so eloquent as the other. He reasoned his points, shewed conclusively to them that the black person was equal to the white with an education. The meeting closed for the evening.

Meeting of School

The next day being Monday, the school opened under propitious circumstances. The first day there were about one hundred and thirty schollars, of all ages, colours and sexes, some young as eight years. There were a fiew urchins at the moderate age of forty five seeking knowledge, some mammas and some that wern't, some soon would be. Then there were all hues from a light orange graded down to a black walnut. Girls dressed as school misses generally, white aprons with pockets in them. Books and pencils to mark with. Their wool had undergone a thorough pulling, to make it strait. Some carrying little baskets on the arm, bonnets or hats to finish their costume for the new seminary.

The boys all dressed in the "Loyal" blue, generally old cast off coats and pants of soldiers. These were graded to the length of boy, nothing to do but cut off the end of sleeves or pants, the balance of course fitted the boy snugly. Old caps or hats as the case might happen. Many of them with satchels (havre sacks) with a primmer thrust in, or something else. Thus equiped, we see them going to school daly. The first day or two there was a great rush for books. It was difficult to get a supply.

There is another school in town, called Pay School. May be called the high. The branches taught here of the doubtful order.

Faculty

Professors: H.A. Patterson, Shemite of Minesota; Brack James, Hamite of Rutherford, Ten.

Assistants: These sallow dish faced, down cast looking women, have the appearance of being disappointed in love affairs 'from the North,' now exibiting themselves by coming to this country to teach the benighted. There are many of that kind following the army, under the guise of doing good.

It will be seen, the school is opened to all appearance, favorably.

At a subsequent meeting for collecting funds for the free institution. the following remarks were made by Professor Brack.

My friends! I have a fiew words to say in behalf of yourself. That they were not chained down now like we used to be, with an overseer, with his breaches stuck in the top of his boots, with a large bull whip after us, drove hard all day, nothing but a little piece fat meat and small corn dodger to eat. (Yankee in the croud, dam them, thats so). No, this battle of Stones River opened up a glorious day on us. It was not the Yankee, as we call them, it was God that took off our chains. We are as free as the birds that flies in the air, and then when we used to come to preaching at night, we had to sculk home, for fear of the patrols. Had to be scringing all the time for fear they would see us.

I had a mistress, have none now. Am as free as she is. Dont have to be running out now two or three miles in the country before day, to be there in time. No that is all past. No overseer to kick us about from post to pillar. We had no time to make any thing for our selves. I acknowledge we had to steal a little to get along, could'nt well help it, but hope the time is past for such things.

It used to be when there was a thanks giving day, the white folks could have their good dinners and we were out in the field with the overseer, with his bull whip after us. But bless God, not so now. We have a chance to enjoy it now. So next Fryday is thanksgiving day. You must all attend.

Now, there is the white folks. If they had their way with us, they would burn down that old Baptist Church, School house, and all of us in it. They hate to see our little children going to school. It hurts them, all most kills them to see it.

But bless God, the day has dawned on us at last. We are on rising ground, free, and on the way to heaven. Great shouting among the redeemed.

My friends, we want to raise some money for the purpose of this glorious cause we are now engaged in. Our school is going on finely. We want money. We want every one to throw in something to help it along.

Prof. takes the hat round the congregation himself, lecture and solicits as he goes, receives the donations. Result of collections, one hundred and about ten dollars.

Who will say that Yankee teachers could not flourish in the South? Here is a demonstration of that fact!

November 10, 1863

An order is out for recruiting negro soldiers at this place, and put them in camp of instruction. Although the Yankees profess not to press them into service, they operate about this way - on Sunday evening a file of soldiers repair to the church door and stand as the negro men come out. They take them in possession, put them in confinement and any other they see about the streets.

They are taken through an examination, such as will make soldiers are retained, the others are let off. They want devilish looking and able bodied negros for this purpose.

When a sufficent number is obtained, are put in squads under drill by some qualified Dutchman.

Passing one morning by one of the churches or barracks, a squad was being drilled by a Dutch officer, who could not speak english plainer than he should, is marching the negros up and down the room. Says to them, Marsh! lep-lep (meaning left foot). No! te odder foot - lep! lep! te odder fot you po tam fool! If you tont lep when I tells you, Ill prake mine sword over your tam wolly head. Halt! Marsh! Now, lep! lep! gis see! You got de odder foot. Take tat mit your tam nonsense (strikes him with the side of his sword).

Such is about the start with them at first. In a short time they get in the way of keeping the step in marching and manouvering. To every appearance make a pretty good Yankee soldier when they are dressed in the "Loyal" blue, but whether they can be made to stand powder and lead is another question. Should not be willing to trust a chance with them, to go through a difficulty.

Now and then hear some of the younger chaps talking among themselves. Bill! Im quine to jine the rigiment next week! What you quine to do in the rigiment? Quine to fite de Reb. Sesesh!

They appear as impudent and as confident of what they will do in the army as many of the "Old Veterans," as the Yankees call the old soldiers that has been serving some time.

At this time there are a greater number of negros coming within the lines than usual, men, women and children. Almost every vacant house is filled to overflowing, seeking their freedom. The fact is the owners generally more disposed to get clear of them, have became so trifling that they wont do any thing at home but eat and sit about, seeming to have lost all energy, if they had any.

Tis hoped the Yankees will get their satisfaction of them before they get through with their phylanthopie feelings for the negro.

There are many now getting rather tired. They say the negros are a lazy indolent set of creatures and wont work without some one after them, driving, but why they continue to persist in their freedom is an enigma. They are not willing they shall be allowed to go in their section of country to live. The fact is they have poor people enough, already there. If they come here themselves to live, their wages will of course, be cut down by having so many more to contend with for employment.

Their argument now is with slavery. In this land a poor white man would have no chance to live. They are not willing to put themselves on an equality with the negro as a slave. Where can be the difference? When they are in competition in labour, both of them working for the most they can get, possibly at a less rate than if one was in the usual servitude.

November 15, 1863

Things here have the appearance of quietness. The farmers bringing in their produce, selling it fast at good prices. The market here is much better supplied than could have been expected, under the circumstances, the country having been foraged so close during the fore part of the year. Wheat good supply, at one dollar for bu. Beef 8 cts, Pork 7 cts, flour three cts, meat one dollar, bu. pototers 1.25, Butter 30, chickens 30, eggs 25, other articles about these rates. Can be seen our condition not so bad at this time as might be expected.

As to stores. The business improving fast. As yet the number of houses are limited. Stocks light, but the sales are generally good, from fifty to five hundred dollars some days. The profits on every thing that is sold is heavy. May average a hundred pr ct. Has been much higher, but competition has reduced it. Freights from Louisville three and a half dollars, from Nashville one dollar for hundred.

Cotton has been raised in different parts of the county, now being sent to Nashville. Sells there at sixty five cts per lb. It helps to bring the green backs in the country, a thing much needed, as little confidence as some have in its abiding faith, is made to represent gold and silver. Fear that is all.

Soldiers going into winter quarters. Quite busy building small houses, and fixing up generally. The Negro Soldiers at the same employment, their camps North of Mr. Carneys house. It was feared they would be an anoyance to the citizens when the thing was first started. Fortunately they are kept close in their camps, both day and night.

The East Ten. Yankees Cavalry had a dislike for that kind of soldier, would shoot at them after night when they had a chance. This cavalry were a hard set of men themselves, some as rough as are generally found, all very bitter against the rebels, if any thing more so than the Northern Yankees. Now sent to some other point, the loss here not regretted.

November 20, 1863

Genl. Bragg has been superceeded by Gen. J.E. Johnson, he having taken the command of the army of the west. Possibly things may change under his management. There is one thing, this army has to labour under too many disadvantages, have too fiew men, are not so well provided with conveniences as they ought to carry on a war successfully. Under all the difficulties, a more daring, brave set of men, never shouldered a musket, are fearless and indifferent to death. The Yankee say their cause is a bad one, deserve a better fate. They meet it like men, let the consequence be what it may. If it were bad in the start, they now feel like they are fighting for their Homes, their property, their firesides, their all.

May be justly said that in almost every general engagement, they contend against superiour numbers, having to expend all their strength at wonce, not able to keep up an advantage when gained.

With equal advantage and numbers, and with the determination, they go in a battle. The Northern men would stand no chance of a victory at any time. Not that the Northern men are wanting in bravery. They are as brave as the Southern men, in a common way. They have not that interest at stake. Their families are at home. Not likely to be molested in case of a defeat in a battle. They know their part of country is at ease. For that reason, not disposed to contend the point at all hazzards, unless odds is greatly in their favor. They are in a general way fighting for dollars and cents. Large numbers would rather the war would continue that stop. Stop the war, many would have no employment at home, or so small that it would look like no pay. Many of these men that are in the army living like fighting cocks, on the best, at high wages. At home labouring hard daly for a small sum, barely respectable (say officers).

There may be a fiew cases with the Southern men in the same line, but rare. They are all willing for the war to stop soon, but are not willing to surrender their point. The Soldiers in each case, are passive.

Small Pox

This disease has been raging here to some extent since the summer. Is mostly confined to the negro population. Some white persons caught the disease, a fiew died with it. A great many negros have fallen victims to the disease. It is a great wonder the plague has not been of a more alarming nature, as there were such a large number of negros in from the country, fit subjects, one in ten who had been vaccinated, and it being almost impossible to keep them from mixing about through one an other. They seem to be like rats, are going at all times and places.

The army had a hospital built for that purpose, on the bank of the river near the Nashville pike. At this place the cases were moved to as fast as they were found out, which is the cause of the disease being kept down.

Being told by one of the negros, who had been sick there, said the Drs and nurses paid little attention, or cared, whether they got well or not. Says as soon as the breath was out, they would lay the dead out side of the door, sometimes lay there a day or two before they were moved or buried, then dug a shallow hole, put them in and cover, not caring how. Are heard to say d-d them, did not care how many died. Some of them almost starved. Large number died.

If this tale be true (as it is the "contraband" evidence, must be so, they dont lie to, or on the Yankees). It shews one of the modes of emancipation of the slave, and making them free indeed.

Government Saw Mills

The saw mills that was established on the river near the R. Road, said to be owned by Gen. Rosecrans and an old partner from Cincinnati, called govt. mills, has been moved to Tulahoma, after having sawed up nearly all the good timber in the neighborhood. From accounts they make a good thing of it. The govt. pay them twenty dollars a thousand feet, laid on the yard. They have got govt. teams, govt. soldiers and negros, belonging to the Sesesh, to do the work thrown in, and the mills, three in number, were modestly stolen from the citizens in the county, for own use.

Who would not want a war to continue when power is invested? These men, if they live, will come out of the war rich, if there is any virtue in green backs.

Monument

The Stones River Battle monument to the fallen officers and Soldiers (Yankee) is now about finished. Hear some complaining among some of the company, that the name of some of their officers is not put on it as they fought as hard and was killed about there too. Of course had a right. But we suppose they will have to be content to have their names inscribed in the "Annals of the Cumberland," a noted book which was published for the benefit of this said monument, and a monument of its self. Any person can satisfy himself by reading the great discoveries made by a certain Col. Trousdale, who was the principle of the secret police, and finally dismissed from service for dishonest transactions, as things subsequently leaked out.

A Yankee Soldiers Profession

At one of the negro revivals of religion, a soldier makes a profession.

After the first feelings of the excitement was over, he undertook to lecture his comrades and negros that was present at the meeting. To his comrades he addressed himself a short time, told them he feared they were disposed to make a sham of the all important matter, warned them of their course, gave them his advice, then turned his attention to the negros.

He says - true, I am a white man, but I have been raised a servant in the North, as you are here. You think your times are hard, but you see nothing what I have seen. Have been a subject of all kinds of drudgery. Have worked in a factory. Went as many times as I have fingers and toes barefoot, when there was sheets of frost on the ground, to work. Had to work the ten hour system at winter time. It would be after night before I got home, had but litttle to eat when I got there. Go to a cold bed, and have to be up by day, get ready to work before it was light, before any of you are up.

This is the way we poor people live in the north. There is hundreds of children living in the same way, young as eight years old, all have to labour hard, and scarcely get pay enough to clothe and keep us from hunger and cold.

My poor mother, who is in her grave, died with almost starvation. If we get sick, could hardly get a doctor to attend us. I joined the army because I thought I could make more that way. You may think your lot hard, but it is nothing to what we poor people have at the north. He went on pretty much in this stream for some time.

November 30, 1863

The Thermometer this morning ranges at 17°. So far, the coldest weather we have had for the last three years. Is generally anticipated we shall have a very cold winter, having had such mild winters for several seasons past.

No news of interest to be heard from any quarter. The soldiers have gone to winter quarters, not likely to have any disturbance until the opening of spring.

Up to this time large numbers of negros have been coming to town, now they are slackning off. Think the Yankees are getting tired, if the truth could be known. They have numbers of negros at different employments. They also see it is necessary to drive them to get work. It is hoped the Yankees will get their satisfaction with the down troddin race.

From accounts - Jno. H. Morgan and the officers that was confined in the Ohio Prison (seven in number) with him, have all made their escape. Has created quite a sensation. Every thing on the look for them. A thousand dollars is offered for their apprehension. Suppose they feel, at Columbus, like the boy who had let his bird loose. The Gen. will have to be verry careful or he may be caught. Yankees will go their death for a fiew dimes. They are worth catching.

Since making the above note - See Morgan has turned up in Virginia, all safe and sound. Has published a long account in the papers how they managed their escape. Is quite a thrilling narative.

Through hair breath escapes from detection, the affair reminding of Baron Frank of his prison feats, in cutting through walls, mineing under ground, to make his escape from prison.

Possibly may hear of Morgan up again and on his rounds, visiting old acquaintance, in some shape, but he will be cautious how they approach him. Another time tis hoped that that may fall in his hands, that he will shew liberality. Brave men are always liberal.

December 10, 1863

Not much said or doing about army movements. Presume they are in winter quarters. Frequently hear of cavalry raids and some fighting in that way. In every case the Yankees report, is they were victorious, that may all be on paper, for the purpose of keeping up an excitement.

Occaisionally see and hear of some of the Southern Soldiers comeing in having got lost and captured. Most likely they deserted. They appear to submit, verry willingly, to their fate. All tell a distressing tale as to the situation of the Southern army. Scarcely any thing to eat, such as poor lean beef, not more than half rations at that, small quantity of coarse corn meal and not enough. Soldiers scarcely half clad and in a manner shoeless. Great numbers threatning to lay down their arms and comeing home.

It must be admitted, the army is in a bad condition, not having the comeforts they should to make them feel like soldiers. But things are not so bad as represented to us. Nearly all we see, that comes within the federal lines, are, to all appearances, warmly clad, some of them better cloths than they were in the habit of wearing at home, the colour being the only objection, having a dirt appearance. They make estimates of what they had to pay for the out fit, coat, pants, hat and shoes, the purchase being made with confederate money. Says one, how do you get the money to make a purchase? as you only get eleven dollars a month as a soldier. Oh! We speculate in the camps, make money that way, buying little things and selling again to the soldiers.

We leave this matter to the better informed on that point to solve the question. It is reasonable to suppose every man that does a thing, he may be a little ashamed of, that he will make up the best excuse for himself he can. No one is willing to own up squarely that he deserted the army.

There are many that say they had no hand in getting up the war and wish those that did, to go and do the fighting, for they wont. This may be true. This class of people scarcely ever go in danger, but they are generally industrious behind the curtain, in bringing on a difficulty, and when fully commenced, most likely step aside and manage to bring the peacible men in the difficulty. They then will have to fight their way out the best they can.

There are thousands, in both armies, who were drawn in against their better judgement, by party leaders and management. In looking over the ground, it appears the minority are in the habit of ruling the masses of the people, although the people profess to be a majority power. We are ruled by force of circumstances.

At this time great exertion is being made by the officers in the Yankee army to get the men to reinlist again, for three years, and as their time is not out for some six or eight months yet, as a further inducement to do so, are offered a furlough home for thirty days. Large numbers rejoining and availing themselves of the home trip. A fiew are disposed to hold back and serve their time out, then quit the business. Rail road cars crouded every day with soldiers for home. This arrangement of course, keeps the officers in their present position, and likely making three dollars to where they would one at home, and a further inducement to soldiers to join, large bounties being offered in money or something else. This is all a money making arrangement, giving employment to large numbers who have scarcely any at home that would pay so well.

There is quite an excitement here now, mostly with the negro regiments. They are taking up all young able bodied men and putting them in the ranks, to be drilled for soldiers. A good many think they will like the employment, but some of them manage to step off. There is quite an encampment of them here at this time. They continue to add to their number every day.

There is a Colonel attached to this regiment, quite a stiff looking fellow. Appears to feel his importance. He is a white man, to all appearance. Would not wonder that under the leather he is an out and out negro. At any rate, he is making money by the operation of being Coln.

But little now said about the "Old Stars and Stripes." It seems a thing of the past and forgotten. No display of fine flags and banners. All absorbed in the negro and negro freedom. They are looked on by some of the Yankees, as a better race of people than the white. Many of them say they do not feel themselves above the negro, and possibly this may be the case, for we see many of them, to all appearance, as much degraded as any negro. But among this class of men we find some that may be called high toned men, and are as much opposed to setting the negros free as any Southern man. This class will, in the course of time, become tainted by association.

A young man (Yankee) whom I had made an acquaintance, was telling me, A negro boy about fifteen years old, came along where he was on picket and stoped. He commenced a conversation with the boy. The boy was pointing out who was "Sesesh" in different directions of the neighborhood, and had a good deal to say. At last he put the question, do you know what a union soldier is? His answers was quite correct. He then asked the question, do you know what they are fighting for? Yes! "They are fighting to free all us black folks." Soldier acknowledged he felt rather humiliated to think it had turned out to be his business to fight for the negro race, in place of the restoration of the Union. If he had heard the word negro mooted, when he was volunteering, he would have stoped, if his name had been half written.

December 15, 1863

We advance the date, but little of much interest to note. We are now having quite a cold spell of weather. The Thermometer has been down as low as 18°, the coldest so far that has been for three seasons. Every thing quite dull, with the exception of the soldiers going home on furloughs. The Rail road is sigularly employed, carrying army stores to the front for the use of the soldiers.

On seeing a small scrap of a flag, dangling by a string on the cupalor of the court house, Murf.

Address

Old Flag — See thee almost forsaken. See thee clinging to the mast like a sailor in a storm, fluttering in the breese, tailless and almost starless. Fear thou hast been taken at an uncanny hour, joined a cause. Thy countrys ashamed, thus neglected in thy age.

Have heard of thee in thy youth. Thou did'ts act nobly, gallant in thy countrys cause at Bunker Hill, taught the enemy the first lesson of thy skill, at Bradywine, was active then too. Led on the brass to battle and to victory. At Yorktown, thou did'ts the noblest deed of all. There, thy enemy acknowledged thy superior skill and surrendered.

Again hear of thee, at N. Orleans, nobly doing battle. Then the proud Brittons were taught a second lesson that will last. Still we follow thee on to Mexico, there thou acted gallantly and nobly to thy enemy, first in and the last to leave the field. On ocean too, hast had many gallant victories, ever ready at thy countrys call. Nations learned to honor thee and proud to call thy name and acknowledge thy power.

But Old Stars and Stripes, what has come on thee of late? Thou seemst depressed. Is it because thou hast destroyed property wantingly in thy enemys country? Surely this cant be it! When thou wast in Mexico, the property of citizens was not molested! by thy soldiers! No mules was stolen. No houses or fences was burned. No one robbed by thee! Hast thou joined thyself to a faction which is now about to deceive thee? repudiating the cause which it proposed to uphold? and turned to abolition and the negro? Dost thou fear thou hast lost thy power by being so neglected. Cheer up! Have loved thee! Would love thee still.

Decem. 10, 1863

Very little has transpired, for some days past, worthy of note. The weather is moderating and more pleasant. Those that are in business are selling a good many goods, considering all the difficulties the pass. Business is quite stringent. All persons that carry goods out of the lines have to procure a permit to do so.

Decem. 25, 1863

This is Christmas day. All quiet. No news stirring. The little boys are amuseing themselves, as well they can. The town is not crouded with the negros as it used to be in their day of slavery. When at this time they did enjoy their freedom, all faces shewed cherfulness and good feeling, asking Christmas gifts. They appeared to enjoy more happiness in six days than now in six months judging from the manner we now see, the fiew mopeing along the streets, no one to care for them. They now seem to have a dull stupid look.

A Refaction of the Past

We are now about to close another year of the war and, to all appearance, are no nearer settling the vexed question than we were two years ago. It has more the look of continuance than any thing else. No offers of peace proposed in any quarter. Preparation still going on briskly. The Yankees are disposed to make money out of the operation. The majority of the officers are doing a much better business by having the war go on.

It does appear that it is the business to kick up every little obstruction in the way, to keep matters in a broyl. Every move, things are made worse. The Yankees are making Secessionists faster than if Davis' government.

Those that were disposed to be for the Union at first, and for some time after the war began, are now the furtherest off, and feel the most bitter against the cause that is now persued. They feel they are treated badly in almost every thing.

This allowing the soldiers to take the property of peaceble citizens, that are not disposed to interfere in any of the army movements, is all wrong, but it is done every day. The Federals have got the negro property, where ever they have been, to be worthless. (We let that pass as they contend that negros are not property). Mules, horses and other stock is property. Why not let it alone? Why not pay the citizens the value of any forage that is taken? They say, the U.S. is able to pay its way, and it is supposed does, to the utter last farthing.

Uncle Sam, as the country is called, has now a sort of fellows engaged, who are stealing both from Peter and Paul, and feathering their own nest handsomely.

Thus they will steal, say it is a war necessity, that they are allowed to subsist on the people. Some times they will pretend you will get pay, will give a receipt to be paid by some officer that cant be found, for about one fourth of what they get. This is done by all sons of contractors. This is the way with the thousands of whose who are allowed to put their hands in Uncle Sams pockets.

They turn round and make out charges for every thing that has been procured, in this way as though they had paid out the money at full rates. Uncle Sam, who is easily duped, or if he knows, lets it pass. Steps forward and foots the bill in a pompus manner, with a kind of stuff he calls "Green Backs," which has cost him nothing more than the paper and printing. From the lavish manner in which he deals with his currency, gives grounds of suspiciou that at some future day, intends to repudiate.

This matter could have been settled two years ago, if proper honerable steps had been taken. The people were more ripe for a settlement at that time than they are at this date. If Genl. McClelland, or Gen. Buels policy have been carried out, which was honest dealing. Unfortunately their policy was unheeded and corruption was permitted to reign, and go into confusion.

We have this day bitter union men fighting in the rebel ranks than can be found in the so called union ranks of the north. They were for peace, on fair and honorable terms, but that had been refused them. Tennessee shewed it was for the union by its vote of sixty thousand. Would have stood firm, but by some change of policy, necessity compelled it to adopt a different course, being compelled to take sides and battle against the Northern Section.

The Southern people may be subjugated, but they will never be conquered. The longer the war lasts, the greater will be the inate hatred to the northern portion of the country. They feel their all is lost, and they are indifferent as to what will be their fate in battle. Death has but little terror to them.

The better postion of the northern people are all at home with comparitively fiew exceptions. The majorities that is in the army are the scrapings of cities and towns who have little or no employment, are willing to engage in almost any thing for gain.

As an evidence of this, a soldier acquaintance in common conversation, told me he had frequently heard the remark made, before they came south and as an argument, why they should come, was the southern people were all rich, had plenty of gold and fine gold watches. Would be no trouble to make as much money as they might wish in a short time. These speeches were made by men who wished to be officers.

January 1, 1864

Last night we had a verry remarkable change in the weather. On yesterday (31), the thermometer was ranging high as 55°. A slight rain came on about night, wind changed round north, continued to get cold fast, and by morning the Thermometer was down to three degrees above zero, a change of 52° in the course of twelve hours. Several soldiers froze to death on the cars on the Chatanooga road, exposed in the box cars.

Tis understood that this change was the same all over the U. States. At the north it was more intense, the Ther. at some places, as low as forty degrees below zero. Some places the snow was quite deep. Many places stock suffered very much, froze to death. Large numbers of sheep lay down, their wool being wet, they froze to the ground.

At this time wood was in great demand. It is understood in some instances at Nashville some benevolent persons charged the moderate price of thirty five dollars per cord, so the papers say. War and cold weather shew the christian feeling of mankind.

Things about Murfreesboro progressing as well as could be expected at this time. There is a fair trade among those that have business. Provision from the country is being brought in liberal quantity, in fact more than could have been expected from the chances of the past season.

Market Quotations

We take a small review of the market here. Of this date Beef selling round 6, pork 6 to 7, Butter 40, Eggs, 40, Bacon 8, Lard 12½, Irish potatoes 200, meal 120, Flour $4, other things in proportion.

Groceries - Sugar 25, Coffee 30, molasses 150, Salt 1250, castings 15, Tobacco, high enough at all prices.

Whisky, an article of prime necessity, 150 black bottle or any price that may be asked. Other articles in the grocery line in proportion.

Dry goods - Calicos 30-60, Domestic goods 45 to 65, articles in that line in keeping with their prices.

Money - Green backs all the go. Union and Planters 40 dis, Bank Ten 45, gold worth 60 premium, Southern money worth 25 in the dol.

Cotton in Nashville 62c. Negros not worth the salt they steal, and a downward tendency in the market.

This is a view of things at the beginning of the year. Many of the above articles on the advance and getting scarce.

Still quote the military, verry stringent in their demands in permits to purchase goods and passes to go out of their lines. Negros are quite a commodity with them. Great exertion used to procure a supply to wait on the gentlemen officers.

We now frequently meet with and hear of others of the Southern Soldiers who have got lost, mislaid, run off or deserted from the army. Well! Dont blame them much. They wanted to come home. All tell a doleful tale about their hardships and sufferings while in the army.

The Yankee Soldiers still going home on furloughs in large numbers. Those that have this privilege have enlisted again for three years. Hospitals here are thinning out. Some of soldiers that has recovered, return to ranks or go home. Large quantity army stores going front, by Rail road, at this date.

Politeness of Pret. Lincoln

An old Lady, who had two sons in the rebel army, taken prisoners by the Yankees. She, wishing to get them released, traveled round and finds them. She takes a trip to Washington to see the Prest. On her arrival, makes known her business to the guard, also she had been a school mate of Mrs. L. This was a passport. She was admitted, escorted by a Soldier.

On her entrance in the white house, finds the pres. alone, sitting by the fire in an arm chair, his feet in another, ordinairly dressed, hair standing like porcupine quill, looks over his shoulder. She advances, makes her business known to him.

Yes! I suppose Jef Davis has sent you here to kill me. Assured him no such thing, as she had never seen Jef Davis. If such should be the case, they would not employ a woman to do such thing. Takes his feet out of the chair, gives it a kick toward her, asks her to be seated. However, grants her petition. She returns, pleased with her good luck and satisfied his appearance would be more becoming splitting rails than sitting in the Prst. Mansion.

The weather has moderated but still quite cold, so far the coldest we have experienced.

Now and then a Confederate Soldier makes his appearance, having lost his way or deserted as usual. They report the Southern army in straitened circumstances, scarcely any cloths or any thing to eat. If that be the case, they cant fight much longer. But we have heard this tale so long that we have come to the conclusion these deserters are mistaken. It must be they apply their individual case to that of the army, which they have left unceremoniously, having to sculk and hide in a manner, starve a little by the way, getting off. Admit it is hard with them, but we will hear all about the thing some future day.

Jany 20, 1864

The Whitling Society is still in existance. Not all of them have other employment yet. Out of said Society now and then one drops off. Still enough remains to carry on the grape vine Telegraph. Some startling telegrams pass over the lines occaisionly about the fights in the neighborhood of Knoxville with Longstreet and others. Grape vine say, the rebels whiped the Yankees badly, took a large number of prisoners, and tis supposed, an expedition will be made in the direction of Kentucky.

The news papers say the Yankees have won the day handsomly, have drove the rebels out of Tennessee. This is about the items we now get. Most likely both lines are thunder stricken, nothing of it, all sensation. Then we hear Gen. Johnsons army is lost. Dont know what has become of it, is on some strategetic move. Something will turn up soon, but little said about the armys on the Potomac. Things quiet there, possibly they may be making arrangements for a fishing excursion next spring. They appear peacible, not disposed to fight, altho the news papers have quite a demonstration of their moves going on.

We hear of some shells being thrown in the city of Charleston, and the Yankees think they have set some of the houses on fire, for they saw some smoke in that direction (very likely). They acknowledge Charleston is rather a hard nut to crack. They make heavy attacts on the place, and have the fortune to withdraw, their war vessels in good order.

It is said there is a large number of negro soldiers stationed in that portion of the country, and they have done some gallant fighting? This is of the doubtful gender.

The Times Chat

Gen. Mc Clelland is spoken of as candidate for President and Genl. Campbell, Wilson County, Ten., Vice, a very good ticket if carried through. They are both high minded, honorable men, no doubt would fill the office with dignity and honor to the country.

Lincoln is also spoken of as a proper man to run for reelection. He has been used as a cats paw for the last three years. From all appearance is willing to submit to the same thing for another term. He and his party have rode the union down, are at this time on the back of the negro, in all probability will with him, go to the devil, for his destination tends that way.

Chase has some aspiration to the Presidency. He is spoken of by the papers as having claims to some of the loaves and fishes. He could carry out the negro system to advantage, being a wool dyed abolitionist. Is a smarter man than Lincoln, more tact in management of affairs, in fact, Lincoln has been a tool in his hands.

Still we have another who is spoken of in the same line, who would wish to save the country from destruction, Jle. Fremont. He too would be true to the cause of abolition of slavery, according to the paper accounts. The Dutch of Missouri are for him to a man, if they can get him nominated for President.

Should these claims be supported would bring the party in difficulty, most likely a defeat, ruin the great scheme of emancipation of slavery, and destruction of the union.

The abolition party are now beginning to look at things in a different light to what they pretended to do two years since, when they were claiming to be fighting for the "Old Stars and Stripes," and restoration of the Union. The South claim to be out of the Union, to this they objected tenaciously. How is it now? If what they then claimed be true, then they stand in danger, they see if the union is restored, they will then be defeated. The South will of course, cast its vote against them.

They are now willing to make a small twist and say, indirectly, the South did go out of the union by the act of Secession. So far they feel safe, and to make the thing look feasible, get up an oath of allegience, or amnesty, to be administered to all, in case of return to the union. Here the matter is still twisted a little further. The amnesty oath is only offered to citizens and soldiers, to all officers in the rebel army, they are exempt. So the thing hangs upon a thread. They know by this move, that the war will be prolonged for a greater period, and in the mean time, manage to bring round an election without any aid one way or the other from the disinfected states.

And when again elected for a second term, they would make the South feel their force and power, as it was with the Egyptians of old, when it was required of them to furnish double quantity of brick per day and find their own straw.

January 25, 1864

As a matter of connection of passing events, still have to lug in the negro character. For this I may hope to be excused, as the negro has of late become a noticable person with a certain class in this community.

Is unfortunate to have to adress to the sayings and doings of the negro often, but as the thing has taken the coarse it has, I shall content myself and follow up the history of events as they transpire. By so doing may in the course of time gleam something worthy of note.

There is still a disposition to press negros into the army service. There are houses full of negros in town, enjoying their freedom, living pretty much as animals (men, women), more than human beings. The Yankees have large numbers living in camp, women and children. Great numbers of them dying every week. The small pox still breaking out among them. As fast as the disease is discovered among any, they are taken to the small pox hospital. It is feared the disease will not be stoped until the increase of negros in this place stop.

February 1, 1864

There is quite an excitement here, to raise cotton. There is quite a number of Yankee officers, renting farms from the citizens for that purpose. We see men anxious to engage in the business, who most likely has never seen a cotton stalk grow. They are paying three dollars per acre. There is great enquirey for cotton seed and paying the moderate price of one dollar per bushel, and willing to buy all that can be found at that price.

I shall be pleased to know they can get a good supply. Want every one that can procure a handful, to engage in the enterprise. No doubt they will make a good thing of it. They came to the country to make money, in some way, and cotton is one of the articles to produce the effect, among the other means. The price now quoted at Nashville, is sixty five cents.

Operation - They propose, in the first place, to pay three dollars rent, do repairs on plantation, to hire Negro men at ten dollars per month and find them in provision, or fifteen dollars, they to find themselves women, the same proportion for their time. Pay half the wages each month, in cash, the other half at the sale of cotton crop.

A negro who is getting one hundred and twenty dollars a year, will having owing to him, at the end, sixty dollars.

A Spy as the Yankees Thought

The ever vigilant Yankees thought they had a good thing on hand, about to trap a spy. It was in the person of a young lady who had come in from the country to have her teeth operated on, and had put up with Mrs. I-s for the time.

Miss R-t is a tall stout and rather masculine appearance. She wore a straw hat and feather, the balance of dress nothing unusual in appearance. However "the boys," as they call themselves, in passing the door took it in their heads that this person was a young man, in the dress of a female. So, on Sunday morning arrangements were made for a "raid or dash," and capture the supposed spy. A corporal and a pretty heavy guard made a flank movement and surrounded the house and garden to prevent any escape.

The old and young lady was quietly sitting by the fire, reading, when the corporal, very unceremoniously, put his head in the door, told he was ordered to search her house for a spy, a man in womens cloths. She assured the corporal no person was about the premises but herself and the young lady. He insisted that it was his duty and must examine. Search was made all through the house, and nothing found. Quite a disappointment. An explanation was had before the provost martial and matters settled satisfactorily. The men looked somewhat like the boy that had let his bird loose accidentally.

Yankee Impudence

A negro soldier, a fiew days since, made a purchase of a watch of a jeweller in town at twenty five dollars. A day or so after, took a notion he had paid too much, wished to rus back, tells the surgeon of the company (who was called a white man, most likely belies his color). He undertakes the case for the negro. They both visit the other shops about town, has the watch valued, then goes to the seller, asks if he had sold it. Said he did. Well! Says the doctor, you have to do one of three things. Whats that says the seller. You will have to refund me five dollars, take back the watch, or have your house shut up! Well Sir, I will do neither. The doctor was taken, all standing at this prompt reply. He did not know how to proceed further, stood a fiew moments more, scratched his head, then he, and his client, made their exit out at the door, grumbling something in the way of threats of arrests.

The watch seller went to the provost martial and stated the case to him. He was told to return to his business as the military had nothing to do with such cases.

So by this, it may be seen how the unsuspecting are frequently imposed upon by those who claim to have the power of the military to back them in their rascality. No doubt in this case, this whelp of a Dr. had proposed a partnership with the negro to swindle the watch seller out of five dollars, thinking he would pay rather than be arrested.

Some Yankees can stoop to such low pitiful tricks to gain a farthing, that they are a disgrace to the name.

Want of Something To Do

Mr. Covington, a quiet citizen of this place, had to submit to have a "house search" made for a Rebel uniform, as the Yankees said they had information that there was one there, or to that effect. This happening at night, the family had, or was about, retiring to bed, when a rap was made at the door. Enquirey was made what they wish? A guard of five men make their appearance. One of the number stated they were ordered to search the house for a Rebel uniform, but his language was such broken dutch, that it was uninteligent and difficult to understand. The lady of the house told him she did not understand what he said. He insisted she did. However they came in. Why did you not come in the day? We go when we please was the reply. One of them represented himself as the assistant Pro Martial, insisted they must not talk so insulting to them. Mrs. C. said she had insulted no one.

The search commenced. Mr. C. shewed them round. They then wished to be shewed up stairs, did so, but no uniform could be found. In opening trunks and boxes in another room, one trunk was found to contain three or four pieces of bed clothing. The search for uniform changes to something else. They want to know why these four pieces was put in that trunk by themselves. Were they not left there by some Southern person for safe keeping? and many such questions as that. Whose carpet is that up here roled up? Answers was given to all the enquiries as to why and where fore's, whether satisfactory or not to them. They concluded to leave, having found nothing they could well take. Mr. C. wished to know their names, one given, but of such dutch character could not be recollected, even if a genuinne name. Before they leave they give Mrs. C. a reprimand in broken language, telling her she must not talk so insulting to Union Soldiers, or they would have her arrested. She had said nothing to insult any person.

They had been through all drawers and boxes and trunks. By this means they see where a person may have any thing valuable they can more conveniently steal, for a large class of the so called Union Soldiers are in the army more for plunder than any thing else. That was principly their mission South - Bummers.

Feby 15, 1864

Things are moving on slow, but little to be seen or heard. Scarcely enough to make an item.

The hospitals at this place are quite full with the sick and wounded from the late battles. We have a pretty good display of the military. Large numbers of the strap gentry are figuring about town, living fast, eating and drinking, no doubt better than they are in the habit of at home. The war does not effect them. As to dangers, they manage to keep out as much as possible. It would be a calamity for it to stop. They would then be ordered home, then take old wages a dollar per day.

The negro regiments are still being increased here in the camp of instruction. They go in squads to the country and collect all able bodied negro men, and bring them in by force. Many join willingly, looking on the thing as a matter of amusement, never seeing far ahead to know what will be the result of the fun. A strict watch is kept over them to keep them from deserting, others are shy about being caught. When it is understood more men are wanted, there is generally a good deal sliping about to keep out sight of the recruiting men. They are in some respects to be pitied. They are misled by the designing Yankees, telling them about freedom and the pleasure they will enjoy. Many now are acting freedom, still a thing they are not capable of comprehending.

The Yankees are getting a capital in the way of Negro Soldiers. They will not know how to appreciate until it may be too late. Instead of giving strength, they are weakening their power, and if persisted in, may be the over throw of the boasted union army. Will only be necessary to get the ranks well filled with this class of soldiers to ensure great defeats. They are mistaken in the negro character. It is contrary to their nature to make good soldiers. As a mass of people are cowardly, not one in ten will do to rely upon. A fiew regiments in an army will demoralize it, and throw it in confusion, and likely defeat.

If what is reported to be in the Federal army of this class soldiers, I would not hesitate to say the Confederates will gain nearly every battle that may be fought and in all probability gain their independance.

Febuary 20, 1864

The small pox still continues prevalent at this place, principly confined to the negro population. Many are said to die at the pest hospital, but this all amounts to emancipation. Get all the black negros out of the way, then the white negros from the south will then come in for a chance to get employment.

We scarcely ever hear these times any thing said about the "Old Stars and Stripes" and the restoration of the Union. The matter appears to be a thing that was, to use their expression, Stars and Stripes, and old flags, has "played out." As an evidence, look on the court house, see the small remnant that is dangling in the breese. Would be difficult for a stranger to say what had been represented there, what was once a neat flag. Constitution too, it is feared, is sitting in some dark corner, bewailing its sad condition. Union has also parted friendship and gone to some foreign clime, to mourn the fall of a once happy country. Law and justice may be found lying loosely round, having been overpowered and vanquished by the Knights of the Straps.

The name Union Soldier has no other signification than to distinguish one kind of men from that of another. Almost any other name would make a substitute, and the most proper one is Abolitionist. This is the principle now being worked upon in all its features.

Washingtons birthday passed off without much notice to attract. These men are loosing fast what little patriotism they had for the father of the country.

Now and then we hear of some desertions from the Rebel army. They always bring in a doleful account, of the scarcity of provision, and the likelyhood of starving in the south. There is one thing that contradicts the statement. All that come in look in good order, and generally well clothed. Take these we see, as samples of starvation in the South, we come to the conclusion that they are lying to the Yankees, possibly to gain favor, as the contrabands do.

We may now say we have managed through the winter. It has been a cold, regular spell throughout, ice having formed on ponds six inches thick, water that was in barrels, froze solid. This is an uncommon occurrance in this climate. The Ther. down as low as 3° above zero. On the night Jany 1st, paper accounts say many persons lost their lives by freezing. Many parts of the country, it is said, the fruit trees are winter killed, to what extent not known.

March 1st, 1864

An Election was held at this place for civil officers. A small vote was given for sheriff and other officers. Some districts no election was held. The oath of amnesty had to be taken before any person were allowed to vote. There was also an oath drawn by Gov. Johnson, which he required to be taken. Some took, others did not. The whole thing being a burlisque on civil law. The election was held in a scattering way, not much legality in the thing.

There is doubts whether any person who swear the election officers are legally authorized to do so. This will be a matter for the future. However they will be qualified to hold most courts, and go through the motion.

On the other hand, how is the civil law to be carried out when the people are so strictly governed by the military. Every person must have a pass to go in or out the lines. Tis folly to say, both can carry on their operation at the same time without clashing. One or the other must cease. From the signs of the times, it is easy to see which will sway. If justice and civil law be allowed to rule, then the military characters would give an endless job in tresspassing, horse and other stealing, and a hundred other petty crimes.

So summing the matter up, it may be said we are hardly enough civilized to have law and order introduced amongst us. We must be content with the savage mode a little longer.

Frank Lazarus

Is a small sized man, light in weight and light in mind, thin visage, wears a nice little sun burnt goatee. In money matters is very close, always feels verry poor. Now when Frank is at himself, is considered a man of means, still he felt himself verry poor. Would make out to keep up appearance with the better class of people.

Now when the rebellion broke out in the year 1861, he like many others, felt verry patriotic, joins a volunteer company, felt like a David meeting a Goliath, and would not hesitate to be found dying in the last ditch, a perfect glow of patriotism pervaded his feelings, was popular enough to be elected Lieutenant to the company. When in his full uniform rig did not stand much above his Sabre. In the ranks he marched and counter marched, and finally marched off to Bolinggreen. Was in the Fort Donaldson battle, was captured as other soldiers were, sent to prison, served his time, was exchanged as others. The boys on reorganizing their company, forgot by some means to elect Frank to his old position as Lieutenant. He plays Sullen, would not go in the company as a private.

He is seen about here during the time Braggs army was quartered at this place. At the retreat he falls back too, but on his own hook, for it appears he commanded no body, and no one commanded him. We loose sight of him, understanding he had gone to Arkansas to look after his plantation and hands, his patriotism having taken the wane. So in this condition of affairs, he is lost sight of, none much distressed about it.

When of a sudden, who do we hear of, but our Lieutenant, bobbing around until he is captured by the Yankees and marched to the court house, a prisoner now, willing to swallow old Ab's and Andys amnesty oaths, having understood these. Will make a good and loyal man, and save his land, which is far more profitable to dying in the last ditch. Report say he had been lying about conveniently in the neighborhood for some time, and it is intimated he managed to have his name handed in. This cant vouch for.

As luck would have it, the guards understood when he might be captured. They got up a squad of five soldiers, repair to the place, meet him just coming in (he and friend), at the critical moment. They nab him, bear him off triumphantly to town, a martyr.

Ah Frank! You are little but you are cute. Do you intend to take the whole dose at once, and be what is called a loyal man, have all the privileges that is allowed the soverigns of this part of the country? You may have a pleasant time. There is doubts about that. You would have better laid in the last ditch a little longer. Your property has nearly all disappeared. At this time you could not have made matters much worse.

Possibly you think you have done enough to establish a name that may be handed down to future generations, for patriotism. If so, hang up your fiddle.

March 5, 1864

The Yankee cotton planters are making preparation for puting in their crops. They are collecting up Negros, horses and farming implements. They appear to pitch in, as though they will make a fortune the first season.

True, cotton is bearing a good price in N.Y. 80c, but every thing else is high in proportion, and those that are engaging in the business have little or no experience. By the time they bring "buckle and tongue together" in the fall, many will find dame fortune has taken wings and "flew away." It is quite likely they will see what "freed" men will do for them at ten dollars per month, and pay for rations at the high rates that provisions are, viz. Bacon 18, Beef 12, meal 130, other articles in fare portion.

Shall note, their operations in farming through the season may gain some instruction from Northern farmers, who essay to come south to teach dull clod hoppers how to raise cotton.

March 15, 1864

Hear of little that is of interest from the armys. The Tel. operators try to keep up an excitement for the benefit of news paper market.

A large number Yankee Soldiers have gone home on furlough, and to recruit their regiments. Numbers are said to have reenlisted for the period of three years.

March 20, 1864

At this date there was a heavy fall of snow at Chatanooga, measuring thirteen inches deep.

The U.S. Government is actively engaged, transporting large quantities of army stores to Chatanooga by R.R., some by wagon trains. There is great quantities of stores also arriving at Nashville, to be sent front to the union army.

Soldiers now returning from home to the army, having been off on furlough, and recruiting their regiments. Fifteen regiments passed through this place, on foot. Was surprised to see them on their way back. Each regiment numbering from one hundred and fifteen to three twenty five, in place of full regiments of one thousand men and officers. How is this?

We see the men lacking. At the same time, all the regiments small as they are, have the full quota of officers. Can it be the difference of Fourteen and two hundred dollars per month? Or is it the officers more patriotic than the men to put down this rebellion and restore the union?

Possibly this question can be more easily answered by some disinterested person.

One other thing that was surprising was six regiments, new recruits, said to be six thousand, which passed through this place (but did not exceed thirty three hundred). However out of the number, one eight was boys from the age of fourteen to eighteen years old, and then there was about one eight of old men from forty five to sixty years of age. This may be the last of Lincolns of three hundred thousand to fill up regiments.

Now without supposing any further, the gist of the thing is this. In the North, there is large bounties offered for recruits which runs up to several hundred dollars. This bounty now becomes an object with some. Thus, there are poor families who have several boys. They persuaid one or more to join the army and take the bounty, the boys a small part, the family get the balance. Thus the boys are sold victims for green backs. Then the old men seen in the ranks, they too offer themselves victims for a portion of the precious green article, hoping it may fall to their lot to get an easy place to while away the time, not that they can. Whether Lincoln or Davis either succeed, they secure their grub and pay. They are easy on the subject.

March 25, 1864

We have been lying in a dormant state for some time past, but little of interest in army movements in any direction. We have just passed through quite an inclement winter. Spring time is just opening, and with it we hear of Gen. Forrest opening his spring campaign, having made a raid on Paduca, Ky. It is said he made a general sweep of things, captured and carried off large quantities of army stores. He effected what he went for. It was done with so much apparent ease at first sight it looked as though it was a previous arrangement that he should capture and carry off the stores he did (and may have been, as the Yankees will go any length for a fiew dimes). His loss of men reported to be slight.

The Yankees contend they resisted to the last extremity. They were greatly overpowered in numbers. Paper correspondance are at their wits ends how to fix up the matter for the union men. They have various contradictory reports about the fight and surrender, which makes the whole matter look as clear as mud.

One of the reports had fixed up that the whole affair had been concocted by Forrest and some Northern commissary to have a large quantity of army stores and clothing shipped to that place. He would come and capture, as per agreement. By this arangement the shipper would get a better price for the surplus goods from Forrest than at home. This is a supposition and it may be a reasonable conclusion, as the Yankee character is calculating when money is at stake.

Now the great difficulty was this, the Federal have a Fort at this place, and they had a large number of negro Soldiers, which they look upon as relyable men. In this they are mistaken. There are very fiew that can be made to fight. They have one capacity which they are true in, it may suit the Yankee character, that is Lie and Steal, but as making fighting soldiers, will be found wanting. It is said Forrest is a negro driver, if so, he understands the management of negros-forts when they are quartered, will be no impediment to him.

April 1st, 1864

Still a fiew union regiments returning from home, "going on the front." They dont have the appearance of having added much to their strength by going home, possibly they may come on after a while, when they are more needed. Hear of no movements, more than a fiew cavalry raids. They are not half so desperate as the dispatches have it.

We may look for something startling after a while, as Gen. Grant, who is commander in chief of the U.S. Army, is getting up a grand program of things. From every indication he intends to "make a spoon, or spoil a horn." Lincoln has given the management of matters in his hands, and is going to rely on Gen. Grants luck, as he terms it. He has tryed judgement long enough and has generally made failures, is now going on luck.

It is thought this is about the last chance. Lincoln has run through his line of Genls and if Grant should fail to make the spoon this next movement, the horn will be split. He will have no more material to work on, unless he falls upon a new program, that is to over haul his black capital (which he claims to have one hundred and forty thousand in the field), and see what he has relyable there, to build a Genl. upon. Certainly out of that number of gallant soldiers a fiew might be selected which an experiment could be made with. At any rate, they can make "army moves."

House Search April 15th, 1864

Quite an excitement was had. One evening a couple of Strap gentlemen became excited by seeing a Confederate flag carried across the street by one of my family as they thought. Enquirey was made of one of the neighboring citizens about what kind of people lived at my house (pointing to it). Not being satisfied about the matter, the next day they had a corporals guard summoned, with an order to make a search for a flag, describing the said flag to be about a half yard square and a white stripe in it. The guard came pitching in at each door, with "we are ordered to search for a Confederate flag."

There has been nothing of the sort about the house, have had no flag. "We were told one was seen here." It is a mistake Sir. The corporal was rather disposed to think there might be a mistake. Says hold on boys. I will go and make further enquirey of the informant, goes. In a short time returns with the information that it was seen waived on the front gallery of the house by three young ladies, and he is ordered to make search. Sir, if you are not satisfied with what is told you, you will have to make search. They go to work, drawers, trunks and boxes are opened to their view. They go to the beds, turn down the cover, piece at a time and then turn over the beds, so on through the house. They find nothing that much resembled a flag.

On opening a drawer, there was a small piece of worsted neting, on a couple of sticks with a small ball of the same, stuck on the end of the sticks, the neting about three inches long. Possibly this may have been what you saw, picking up and shewing them. No, that is not what was represented to us, however a thorough search was made. They appeared to be disappointed in not being able to find the flag. They gave up the search, returned and reported nothing found.

The Sequel - One of the family had been across the street with the small piece of worsted net work that was seen, was returning with it carelessly in the hand. It was all red and about three inches long. About the same time, the two shoulder strap gentry was passing. This was the thing that so much frightened them, they took alarm, thought it was a confederate flag. It magnifies from three inches to about a yard square in the course of a fiew minutes. They, no doubt, had heard of such a thing as a "Sesesh flag," had been taught to fear it as a dangerous thing.

Thus we see the gallant "Straps" will at times allow shadows to alarm them. "The Boys" know when a thing is dangerous, or think they do.

Miss Lucy Verner

A superanuated old maid, of some forty five years or more, has an old style in appearance of a sorrowful ill natured look, having acquired it from her habit of ruling the children of the neighborhood, having followed the avocation of school teacher for many years. She is of Northern birth, came to this part of country, was largely patronized by Southern people, in fact, made her what she is, in a pecuniary point. Was liked well enough, and considered a good citizen.

When the war broke out in 1861, she was still living among us, was at a loss what to do, shewed a disposition to play fiddler to both parties. As the Southern feeling at that time was dominant, she took an active part on that side, contributed her mite, in that way shewed as much patriotism as the most of them. At the time, still she had her fears she would not be thought strong enough for the South, although she claimed to be as good a Southern woman as any. She appealed to one of her friends to know what was best for her to do, to shew her devotion to the cause. "By all means madam, hang out a flag at your window," as it is a common thing at this time, for public institutions to shew where they stand.

At this time she had a verry good school going on, of young Ladies in her academy (which she had taken a lease for a term of years). Things moved on and in the course of time the armys began to be quartered about this place, first the Confederate, then the Federal, the latter remaining some time among us. Nothing of importance transpired at this time. No one was molested by either army, however all the schools were discontinued, the Colleges being taken and fitted up for hospitals.

About this time Miss Lucys patriotism began to fade a little, although she had taken a sick confederate soldier to nurse at her house, from the Forrest raid. Thus matters moved on, until the fall of 1862. It became necessary for the Federal army (who had been occupying for some time past), to evacuate the place. At this time she makes it convenient to visit her friends at the North. She closes up her house and leaves, the last we hear of her for some time. The Confederate army again occupy the town. Her house was taken and occupied by some of the officers, but little destruction to her property at first. By frequent of occupants, articles was missing.

After the Stones River battle her house, as numbers of others, was used for hospital purposes by both armys. Her furniture and clothing became scattered, but little help for it, as almost every place was used as a hospital.

During the summer following, Miss Verner returns from the north. She is unable to get possession of her property, leaves for Nashville, then a friend gets her to take charge of his house as he and family have to leave by Military order from the Federal Command on account of Southern sympathy. Miss Lucy, by this time, has turned out to be a Union Woman of the most approved quality, feels like she is entitled to hold the house (the friend had let her go in), against his consent. He had to law her out on his return. She is defeated, "falls back in order" to Murfreesboro, gets an order for her house to be returned to her. Now on the strong side. Sets about collecting what she can of her scattered property. Makes an attempt to have lived off the citizens, enough to repair her loss of property, when they had all undergone the same misfortune, in consequence of the occupation of the army. She goes round among the negros, to find out from them who had taken any thing of hers, with insinuating remarks and threats of what she would do. Fortunately, she did not get her wish put into execution.

She is now reestablished, to all appearances doing well, generally patronized by southern right (or Sesesh as she may call them). Her patriotism now as strong the other way to what she started out with. Is now a key, or refference, when the Yankees wish to find out any thing about the standing or character of any the citizens. She can give the proper coloring to any thing that is necessary. A Sesesh flag would now look as odious in her eyes as the "Old Stars and Stripes" did times past.

Time and circumstances worketh many changes.

April 10, 1864

Little of interest to be seen or heard of at this time. Still large numbers of Soldiers going to the front, having been home on furlough. Their numbers do not appear to have increased. What we see claim to be veterans. All are called veterans who have served some time in the army and have reinlisted for another term of service.

The thing has now settled down as a plain Negro War. Nothing else claimed for it. It is contended that the negros should be free, whether it will mend their condition or not. The abolitionists have set in to accomplish the job. They have the soldiers hitched in the traces, are determined to make them work, whether they like or not, although we see large numbers of the soldiers who are opposed to having any thing to do with the negro question. Are anxious for their time to expire, so they can quit.

News papers have little news of a startling nature. Still keep up a regular number of dispatches. A great many movements reported to take place. They have now got Grant in the neighborhood of Lee in Virginia. Dispatches are having Lee moving round in an uneasy manner. The Yankees are now "on to Richmond," which has been the cry at least a year past.

One would suppose Charleston was now lying in a heap of ruins by the number of shells that has been fired in that direction. They have Fort Sumpter a pile of brick and morter, for they can see through it with their spy glasses. Still the Yankees are a little fearful to go and claim their game. The thing is not quite dead, does still shew some signs of life. They find those rams and torpedos devilish things to meddle with, have caution enough to keep at a proper distance.

April 15, 1864

All the negro soldiers have left this place, have moved their camps to some other quarter, possibly where they may be of some service. It is doubted whether it will be in the capacity of a soldier. They will do to make a shew in that way, nothing else. They are not the material for fighting the regiment. Was about five hundred strong to all appearance. Better looking men than the generality of Yankees. Should they depend on them for a fight with guns, will be wofully disappointed. From the general impression among the Yankee Soldiers is these black regiments will be placed in front of battles to form breast works. Should this be the case, we may hear of defeats of the Federal army.

The best way the negros should be armed would be with spade and picks as privates on fortifications. In this capacity they would be more at home. Their service would tell to some advantage. This is the place they should be, if meddled with at all, but this is the question with the Yankees, who think they have the right, of course they use it.

The contraband camps are being thined out to a considerable extent. Women and children are being sent to some other quarter. A large number have gone through a course of the small pox. Numbers have died with the disease. The remaining on hand about here are not worth the sale they use, are disposed to be idle and collect together and live in hovels. What little they make have no disposition to be saving of, will spend all for something to eat and dress themselves. Have a great passion in this way.

The female portion, when in full dress, have a nack of captivating the Yankees. They have a great disposition to associate together. Negro is quite the thing with Yankees, still they deny they have much love for them.

Cold Weather

We have had cold, clowdy weather for some time past. The season is quite backward for croping.

Today, 11th, we have had a slight snow, a little rain and sun shine all together. Makes quite a mixed day. Pleasant to have fires of mornings.

Business is improving. A good many goods are being brought here and sold at the same time. It is difficult to get them, there being a rotten permit system to be gone through, which makes it unpleasant to do business. Necessity compels persons to submit, for the purpose of making a living. Nothing else can be expected, for should large amounts be made, in the way of money, it is uncertain whether it will be worth any thing in a short time. Green back money is depreciating almost every day. At this time gold is seventy pr. ct premium, cotton advancing, sixty eight cts. It is supposed our Yankee cotton planters about here, can see the green in the article. That is a matter that may be tested some time about the last of the season.

But there is one consolation with the Yankee planters. Should cotton not make a "good stand," they can "fall" back in good order and abandon the plantations, leave the debts, take care of themselves, acknowledge that they were "overwhelmed" at least two to one, let an "investigation" be called.

April 20, 1864

Many regiments still passing through this place to the front. They are small in the way of soldiers, but to all appearance full in the way of officers, the latter know which side of their bread has the butter.

Something will be done before long. Some body will get hurt. Gen. Grant is going to operate in Virginia. He is on to "Richmond," or some where about there. Gen. Lee will have to stand from under or he will be knocked over this time. The "hero of Vicksburg" is after him. Gen. Sherman is after Gen. Johnson with a sharp stick. If numbers is all that is necessary to win the day, the thing is up with Johnson, Sherman has got the men.

H.A. Patterson

This christian individual has advertised a large sale of abandoned property, belonging to citizens of Murfreesboro and neighborhood.

Mention of this creature has been made before in the course of notes, but at no time with a pleasurable sensation. He claims to be an agent of the U.S. for abandoned property, how much Uncle Sam will be benefited by his agency is a matter of question. He is a true live Yankee. Has followed the army under the guise of religion, claiming to be a chaplain, but not much interested in the matter further than to carry out his designs of robbing the people of their substance and applying it to his own use. He is an abolitionist in the fullest sense. The day will come when his doings for the past eighteen months will roll up before his eyes, like mountains - Methodist, as he claims to be.

Well he has collected a large quantity of such property, as furniture, house hold goods, carpetings, large Looking glasses, Family portraits, Law and missellaneous Books, in fact every thing he could lay his hands on which he calls abandoned property. The best of all these articles disappeared mysteriously before the sale, without giving any person the chance of making a bid on them. It is said he has sent them home for his own use. Law Books, he considers an article of value to himself. He is a man of energy in this business. He gets his information from the negros, where any thing may be found. When he finds the place, goes to head quarters, gets an order and corporal guard, demands what he wants in name of the U.S.

At one time in his raids on property, he was headed in his operation in stealing Mr. Keebles Books, out in the country, which was a large library, principly Law Books. This he wanted much. Makes his arangement, goes out with his guard, demands the books. The owner of the house was not at home at the time, but some one of the family was. He was not disposed to let the books go. Is told if the door is not opened they will knock it down. Upon this demand, the key is produced, the books taken, but in this case the books were counted and recipted for.

Shortly after, the man come home, claims said books. They were refused to be given up to him. He makes application to head quarters at Nashville, gets an order for the return. This government agent had to refund with a bad grace, packs up and returns. At this he complains, threatens to resign if the property of Sesesh had to be protected in that way. But he did'nt resign.

Another case, Mr. Henderson, who owned a library of Books of a religious character, which he valued highly, many of them rare and hard to be replaced. Besides this, the library was worth to the owner some three or four hundred dollars. A bidder wishes to have a chance to buy, an hour was agreed upon they will be sold, so he may be there. He sells an hour sooner, takes a fiew of the books in his arms to represent the library as a sample, the whole up. A bid is made by some one. He makes a bid and knocks them down to himself at the liberal sum of Seven Dollars and fifty cents, then passes on to the next article. This is what one Methodist preacher will do to another.

Where is the moral to this transaction?

Property of Mr. Palmer, Ransom, Burton and Crocket, and numbers of others, which this pious man is disposing of in a christian manner. One or two cases the wives of owners of property were present at the auction. It made no difference.

The negros were supplying themselves with furniture he sells, several Pianos, belonging to the Sole College. How the Yankees can make a public institution to be guilty of Treason and sell the property is a question hard to solve. So it was, the articles were sold. Pianos sold, some low as sixty dollars a piece, one fourth their worth.

Such sales as this is little calculated to assist the U.S. out of debt, when it is said its expense is about one million a day. Mr. Patterson will have to dispose of a good many librarys to pay the public debt at the progress he is making. He is looking round for houses owned by Rebels, these he claims to rent out for the benefit of the govt, the occupant must pay to no other person but him.

This system has to be submitted to by the citizens, as the bayonet stands between man and man, one of the modes of making "a union stronger than ever."

It is one of the restorations more bitter to take than the XXX Plantation bitters.

Shall dismiss the individual for the present, necessity will cause a further notice, as something new is transpiring every week.

Genl. Forrest

This man has become a terror to evil doers in the west. To all appearance roams where he pleases, has taken the west end of Tennesee, and north Missippi as his range. From accounts he deals with the Yankees, whether they deserve the treatment will leave for him to say.

In his rounds, he discovers a Settlement, as he supposes, rather encroaching on his teritory, called Fort Pillow. The right of Settlement shall not question. Forrest objects. So about this date he rides up, makes a formal visit to the inhabitants of said Settlement, sends in his card, in the shape of Flag of truce, to surrender the ranche on penalty. He finds this a mixed mass of settlers, such as Dutch, Irish and Conneticut Yankees, and heavily seasoned with "loyal negros" called "color'd people." Now these inhabitants not having the fear of god or man, are found bearing arms, in a beligerant attitude.

Forrest, through politeness (or something else), send another card (as they had not heeded his first call), with a more pressing request, and what he would most likely do if they did not accept of his proposition, as he had the means to carry out his wish.

They stubbornly refuse to receive Forrests invitation. He forthwith orders a march into their quarters, and there beat and thrashed about for some time among them. Report says by this treatment he caused the death of a large number of the inhabitants of the place, both white and black, so much that a portion of the publics were disposed to call it a Massacre of the Citizens of Fort Pillow. They tell strange tales of the affair in the news papers, speak of retaliation, but how is this to be done? by Grierson, who they say, is on the trail of Forrest and who is always careful to keep a respectful distance from him?

However, some reports was liberal enough to say Forrest did not massacre all that he might, but was generous enough to hail a boat and have those that was wounded badly, put aboard and sent up the river. The most strange dispatch stated that Forrest was so cruel to the negros, he caused five (some of them wounded), to dig a hole or grave, when done, pushed the negroes in alive and buried them. Some dispatch say they Scratched out, went to a hospital up the river. To make the matter look more horrible, say he had the negros rolled in the river, shot. Some that was in the water, hanging to logs to keep out of sight, some put in a house and burned. Thus the accounts goes.

There is one thing evident. Forrest must have been there and made a scatterment among the inhabitants of the place.

Note - Out of 700 men in the forts, 400 of them negros, prisoners, 128 white, 34 negros, the latter was full of dutch courage (whiskey), singing "rally round the Flag," when Forrest dashed in among them. If they had pulled down their flag immediately, likely there would have been but little blood shed, but they were so much confused, they forget they had a flag flying. So it was the flag was up, the battle raged until some of Forrest men lowered it for them, hostilibities then ceased.

Forrest did send a flag of truce for the surrender of the place, which is admitted. It was not accepted, no attention paid to it. He had a right according to the usage of war, to take the fort by any means that lay in his power. It was legitimate. Those that were in of course knew what would be the consequence, if they persisted in their resistance. They did resist. Forrest took the place.

The idea is repudiated that he committed the atrocities that he is charged with, by letter writers, of "massacreing all indiscriminately."

April 25, 1864

A Cavalry fight is said to have taken place between Wilder, fed. and Gen. Wheeler, near Dalton, Ga., which lasted some time without much damage to either party. Wilder had to fall back, and from the dispatches we take it for granted he was greatly overpowered, "fought at least three to one, but did it in handsome style."

Also hear of a navel battle in N.C. with gun boats. The Gun Boat Rebel Ram said to have sunk. Three fed. gun boats. If this be the case, which is also granted by dispatches, the boot is on the other foot. One rebel to three federal. From accounts they retired in bad "order." Of course some was killed. They did not have time to count, in the hurry to get away.

Again we hear of a heavy battle on Red River between Gen. Banks fed. and some Confederate. The account we get is rather mistified by correspondents. The suming up of the matter, the federal army was badly defeated. In this case, they had not made arrangement for such thing. The best information we have, they were more interested in capturing cotton bales than they were rebels. Was thought to be more money in the operation. We may set the matter down, as it turned out quite a disaster to the Yankees.

We also hear of disturbances in different parts of Missippi, among the Yankee planters. Now and then raids is made by Confederate cavalry, which proves to be a source of great anoyance to the cotton planters. If this thing is not put a stop to, it is doubted whether the planters will be able to put a "green back" in their pockets this season. They are generally ordered to pull up sticks and go home to the North as they (the rebels), dont wish any cotton raised, and should they be caught there again, most likely some of the neighboring limbs of the trees will have to bear the responsibility. This appears hard and may be just, particularly with men who are so anxious to restore the union by occupying the premises of other men.

To all appearance, Gen. Grant is quite active in getting his army in order. Every thing in his line is on the move. The R.R. Cars are generally crowded with Soldiers and army stores, pushing to the front, both in the army in Virginia and the South West. He is now invested with the whole command of the armies of the U.S. When he gets all matters fixed, he will then make one grand move with all his forces at the same time, and make a general sweep of all Rebeldom, or he will make one grand failure. Should the latter take place, the war may be continued, or the U.S. will conclude a treaty. This would be the most sensible thing. If a war is continued, the country will be entirely bankrupt.

May 1st, 1864

The last fiew days nothing of importance has transpired. Things about Town is quiet. Soldiers continue to go front, but this is a common occurrence. Business has improved greatly for some time past. Our merchants, with their small stocks, goods, are driving a pretty fair business. The weather continues a little cool for the season of the year. Vegetation is a little backward. The farmers are doing what they can, with their limited means, for business. Their horses are scarce and generally in bad order. Produce of every description still continues to advance. Cotton has an upward tendency in the eastern market, now quoted eighty 80 cents. This is about the sum of things at this date.

July 4th, 1864

The day was celebrated by firing thirty four guns at the forts. Beside this no other display by the military. People were attending to business, such as had permits to do so.

What the white people was lacking in patriotism the negros made it up. They undertake to celebrate the 4th, making quite a display. They were in from all quarters. The women were appearantly dressed within an inch of life, with finery procured by hocus pocus on leaving their homes, moving about in shoals, with parasols and fans in hand, putting on lady airs, scarcely knowing common white folks.

The business was to celebrate the day of independance. They were of all hues and colours from the oldest to the youngest. The schools turned out to the celebration. Six picnics in the neighborhood of different religious denominations. Brack heading the Methodist school. His pupils dressed in the best style, with sashes and ribbons, marching with a banner and small flags along the line. They move to Maneys Spring where a stand is prepared and a table filled with the best the times afforded. Candys the staple article. At this place it was called a pay dinner. All that partook "forked" over the dimes. No one backward. Cash plenty.

They gathered at the stand. A Yankee orator mounts, moving off in a flourishing speech, contrasting their present condition to the past, the pleasures of freedom and what they may be. No distant day. A great and inteligent people. The chains of slavery now off their shoulders.

The speech over, dinner is announced. The orator at the head of the table. At a given signal all fall to. Candys, cakes, and other good things disappear as chaff before a wind. After dinner speaking continued. A colored gent mounts the stand and led off in his peculiar style, lauding the friends from the north for what they had done and how the colored people ought to love them for it.

By the time the speaker concludes, things are cleared away and preparation made for a dance in which the colored circle engage and continue to a late hour, intersperced with many loud hoo-pees and ha ha's, thus ending the celebration of the 4th. The Methodist School at this time numbering about one hundred and fifty schollars.

Things About Town

The Soldiers were having an easy time when off picket duty. They cook, eat, and make rings and trinkets, trading in watches, tight rope walking, going to negro meetings at night, working off time the best they can.

Citizens generally sitting about in groups discussing news, smoking, and whitling, a news paper generally on hand. Contents commented on freely. If a Yankee pass or stop at these gatherings, conversation is suspended untill he leave. It was known secret spys were about so it was necessary to use caution to save trouble. One was caught eave droping at a house where some young persons had gathered to amuse themselves at night.

Soldiers passed much of their time making cedar walking canes of wood taken from the battle ground. Officers also had a mania making small desks of cedar off the battlefield.

Revival of religion among the negros was continued day and night. At the close of each meeting near the whole congregation would get up a shout. To all appearance they were on the way to heaven, one brother telling another, "what a happy time we are having at meeting." Yes, I heard of it. You was all drunk on it. I wants to be thar the next time you meet, and I'll be with you too, if the Lord be on my behalf. Yes, dat is de way in de ole times, when de Lord was on the yeath. Da cuse dem all bein "drunk on de new wine, when he was guine to leave de yeath."

It is hard to distinguish a white lady from the colored unless you see the face, they being dressed fine as cloths can make them, gloved, fan, and parasol in hand. Some in deep mourning, all aping the airs of ladys of fashion. These out-fits was generally at the expense of former mistress. Frequently of evenings these ladys may be seen on horse back with long flowing skirts, hat, and feather bobling in the air. They move off in a lope, in company with a colored gent, who had cultivated a mustash, dressed in blue blouse, or coat, buskin gloves, on an evening ride.

Both sex torture their wool to make it grow long and strait. A great passion for trinkets, the more fashionable with near a dozzen of rings on their fingers. A watch is a fashionable article with them. Such is the appearance and doings of negros at this time. They were indebted to the Yankee for this branch of education.

Many of the citizens submitted to take the oath. They were not permitted to do business without.

About the 25th of August a white soldier was shot by a negro passing the streets after night. In an ambulance with two soldiers, one of the soldiers for mischief, hurrad for Wheeler and Jef Davis. About the same time one of them was shot. This takes place at the crossing of the streets near Dr. Baskette, Cricket, and Dr. Claytons houses.

The soldiers hearing this was verry much incenced, thinking it was done by some rebel. They swear vengince and were determined to burn the house of one and hang the other. They were in the act of carrying out the threat but were fortunately stoped in time.

Atrocity of Yankee Cavalry

In the neighborhood of Milton two cavalry forces meet. They have a warm skirmish. In the fight a confederate soldier was wounded, unable to get out of the road. The enemy pass him. In a short time return. They find him still there. He begs them not to hurt him more. As he submitted they curse and deliberately shoot and leave him dead in the road. The captain of the Yankee Squad was a home made Yankee.

In the course of time the rebel cavalry was in the same neighborhood skirmishing round. By some means they capture the home made captain. As a retaliation for killing the confederate soldier he is taken to the same place where the killing was done. He is hung on the most convenient limb of a tree, leaving him there after sticking a note to his coat stating why it was done.

Wheeler Raid Sept. 1, 1864

It was known Wheeler was making a raid cross the country with a large cavalry force, but not thought by the citizens he would reach this place. However, the feelings of the Yankees became strong to a high pitch, knowing their weakness at Murfreesboro, their available men having been sent front. The remaining mostly convalessent solders at the forts for defence, some limping about, arms in slings. Some with heads tied up, and other inabilities. Rather a lame stock for protection, yet enough of able men to do duty. Having a lame look, but disposed to keep up appearance by making threats of what may be done in case the rebels come to town. They would blow up every house with shells, hospitals excepted. This was said to scare the citizens. The tale had been told so often people had became indifferent as to blowing up.

The Post Commander had moved his quarters to the fortification. Still having a slight weakness in his mind as to his safety, he set his wits to work. Monday news—Wheeler advancing on Murfreesboro with a heavy force cavalry. Some times the report, they were not more than four miles off. He kept a constant look out with double pickets out day and night. All stores and amunition moved from town to the forts. This operation, at first, was quietly done to keep down suspicion of alarm, but the mention of Wheeler still advancing. It would cause things to move more brisk.

Tuesday—Excitement getting a fever heat about the forts. This feeling was to some extent in town. A fiew merchants commence boxing goods. The fiew Yankees remaining about town, when speaking about Wheeler or any thing connected, kept a sharp look up the east street, thought to be the way he would make his appearance. They would frequently remark, "I wish he would come on. We would give him h-l." At the same time having the appearance of running at the snap of the finger.

The negros began to suspect things were not right. They had been moving plunder about for two days in different directions, undecided where to go. These movements were going on to about 4 oc. in the evening, when an order from the Genl. was read at each door round town, by a soldier who appeared scared half out of his wits, announcing, to all citizens and non-combatants to leave the town immediately as it will be shelled in case the enemy come in.

This created quite a sensation among all parties. Things now began to move in earnest. Store keepers now busy packing up their goods. In a hurry for a move. Those that had no goods thought to make a strait line for home as a better place of safety, taking chances being shelled out, as threatened by the genl. Some were moving along the streets without any purpose in view, having a vacant stare on the countenance. Negros hurrying on, with bundles on their heads, going in the direction of the forts for safety. On arrival the guards will not admit them. They start again, to some other point. Wagons going all night, moving plunder of some kind.

A Jew, in great anxiety, wishing to get in the port of safety offered a government teamster five dollars to take three boxes goods to the forts. Soon as they can be packed, the soldiers start with the goods after night. They manage to drop off two of the boxes on the way. They arrive with one package, can give no account of the other two. "Did'nt get it." Jew in a quandary. Goods and five dollars gone and no time to investigate.

During the evening now and then Yankees would dart out in the street and strain their eyes up the road. Others on the court house dome on the look out. Thought they could see a large force advancing. Every thing worked to the highest excitement with the soldiers expecting every moment to be attacted by the rebels when night came on. Morning came and every thing was calm and quiet as a grave yard, but fiew to be seen on the streets, and Wheeler not yet in sight. "The grape vine" now commence throwing off some exciting dispatches (a term for uncertain news), which was to make the Yankees feel as uneasy as they were disposed to make the citizens, by offering to shell the town.

Gen. Vancleave at the forts in a feverish condition. Knowing his weakness for defence, he casts about in his mind what to do in the extremity. After consultation it was thought proper to call the citizens out in the capacity of soldiers, armed with guns, by this means evade an attact. So this course was adopted.

Call for Recruits

A squad of soldiers were ordered to go in haste to all the houses in town and summon every man, without respect to age, to report at the court house immediately.

A hint of this had spread over town, creating a new sensation among the citizens. It was rats to your holes. A vigerous scouting operation commenced, running and dodgeing all directions. Many appeared willing to find a hole and pull it in if possible after them. One young man over six feet high, was caught in a garden doubled up with a dry good box over him. One found in a cistern, standing on a ladder, the lid turned down. When discovered says he, here I am! Well, come forth. We want you! A third was fortunate to escape being caught, being secreted in a parlour of a neighbor. Thus, things was managed during the collection of recruits and singular enough too. A fiew middle aged men was taken. They had the appearance of manner being over ninety years of age, hobbling on to war. They were subsequently discharged, for age and inability. Several old men were ordered direct to the forts. They were permitted to march by themselves, taking them the whole evening to go a little over a half mile. They were also released.

The greater part of the day was taken up collecting recruits. The Yankees determined to have help of some kind, to keep the rebels away. In this matter they shewed a disposition to compound with rebels, as they are known to be devils to fight.

Fast as the citizens are collected they are taken to the court house. When a sufficient number come they are formed in line, with an officer to command. At the word March, the company move in the direction of the forts, at which place the new recruits arrive after a dusty, hot march. The genl. was there walking the platform from one end to the other, appearantly much exercised in mind. The genl. location was a large warehouse about one hundred and fifty feet long, in a small hollow near the R. Road bridge and river. At this place there was several prisoners from the court house and pyramids of boxes of goods, the result of last nights movement, the owners guarding.

The men were detained in front of the warehouse about one hour in the hot sun before a proper disposition could be made of them.

Description of Regiment

The regiment took the name of Bloody Hundred. It was made of several nations, Jews, gentiles, a fiew so-called union men, a good sprinkling of "Sesesh," the latter the most numerous. The regiment numbered one hundred men, a temperary surgeon, and chaplain, as a matter of form. However, there were many complaints and excuses offered to be released. In this case the surgeon made partial examinations. Matters for a time was considerably mixed. In the confusion of things two dutch women make their appearance, on a hunt for their husbands. They came in a distressed whining manner, begging their release from service, saying, de Sesesh is jus two miles down te road here. Te will kill you. I wont see you no more. Boo-hoo-hoo! What shall I do! Te will kill you! However, it was no go. They were compelled to fight, to te pitter end.

This regiment was divided in four companys with a captain to each. They were taken through a course of drilling with intermition, untill evening, it being verry warm weather.

Each man is furnished with a gun and amunition, and all other exceteras, to make an outfit of a complete soldier. After night they are marched to town and required to furnish rations at home, then return to the forts, taking up quarters there. This process kept up for three days. The time Wheeler was in the neighborhood. At the end of the time, the guns and equipments are returned, men marched to town and discharged from service.

The post commander appeared greatly relieved when it was known Wheeler had passed on. (A Yankee officer was heard to say while these men were armed it was rather a hazzardous thing for Gen. Vancleave to arm so many rebels in the forts. They could do great harm. He would not be willing to trust them.) Goods were returned to town and business resumed its common way.

Forrest Raid Sept. 30, 1864

Information comes to Murfreesboro. Forrest is crossing Tennessee river with a heavy force of cavalry. His destination, this place. Every thing in the military way is on the move. The same scene of Wheeler enacted over, of packing goods and moving to the forts. The post commander was not idle. He was cautious enough to have the government property secured in the forts, out of reach of raiders.

In the evening he sends a man round. He goes leisurely, not to shew any excitement, with a verbal order. For all business men to quietly pack their goods, to have them ready to move at a moments warning should Forrest come in town. The old cry it will certainly be shelled. The next day an excited order came for all to move goods to the forts. Every thing was in motion, boxes tumbling out of doors and on the move. Load after load, moving to the forts, where they were piled for about a week or more under guard.

The people about town. Nothing to do but walk about, whittle sticks, smoke their pipes, and work the "grape vine telegraph" for exciting news. The guns in the forts were placed in position, pointing on the doomed city, to be let loose in case of an entrance, to go up or down or shelled to pieces.

The negros in an uneasy situation, having a great dread of Forrest. If he come what were they to do? He was thought to be a dangerous man, especially with negros found with blue breeches. To meet this emergency all old corners were overhauled to resurect old butternut coats and pants. When found they were in them in short order, looking quite natural in appearance. They were disposed to claim a master as a protection to them. Many would say, "if he comes, I b'longs to you, hav bin home all de time." The Negro Schools and preachings were suspended for a time.

There being a sufficent number of soldiers on hand, the citizens were not called on to help as in the former raid.

The excitement was on tip toe for about a week. News came there would be no raid on the place, as the cavalry had turned another direction. The post commander's nerves at this news relaxed and more at ease. He sends out an order to the owners of goods they may resume business again. Thus, concluded the anticipated Forrest raid.

A Remarkable Man—De Witt Smith

At the conclusion of the Forrest raid in this part of the country a most daring circumstance took place. A young man (De Witt Smith) and associates from the rebel army, came in the neighborhood of Murfreesboro. Smith called at the house of an old man named B. He was not in at the time. Being called he came and was met at the gate by Smith. Without many words deliberately shooting and killing him dead. Several shots were fired all taking effect. The family is then ordered to leave the house immediately. Fire is placed to the building. It burns to the ground.

It appeared the old man was styled a union man, one who talked a great deal. It was intimated he carried news, giving information to the authorities in town of the neighborhood movements.

The body of the dead man was taken to a son-in-law for buriel the next day (Sunday). A coffin was procured. The undertaker going out with it in his hearse. For company he takes two men, H and C. They going to the place of buriel, are making preparation for interment. Just at that time Smith rides up to the house and dismounts, walks in. Going to where the dead man lay, he deliberately turns him about to examine where he had shot him, which proved to be many times. Then calling for wood, with an oath swearing he will burn him up, ordering all out of the house. In the mean time a neighbor man came in, contending it shall not be done. By reasoning the propriety and like consequence of such course, Smith was finally prevailed on not to interfere further in the matter. The man was finally put in a proper condition and buried.

Young Smith still roaming about the neighborhood, a terror to many, giving out word he will retaliate on any one who may interfere. Remaining about a week. After he disappears, it was believed by the Yankees there were more than a hundred men of the rebel army not far off that were backing him in his course, sending him forward to draw them out.

In a day or two a cavalry force of forty men was sent out scouting for young Smith. They did not meet him, nor any wish to do so, their feeling some one would be killed if they come in contact. Smith appeared to place little value on life. Of course they did. They feared he would pitch in their ranks. Likely kill several before he would be killed. He was known to be well armed all times. These things considered, the scouts contented themselves by keeping the road not far apart with the appearance of hunting diligently. In their travels they find the bodys of the two soldiers shot by Smith. They bring the men in. They are buried. Feeling verry indignant over the affair.

They make a trip or two more out in that direction to search but not zealously, finally give up the job. However, at one time their search was extended far as Windrows camp ground. One night thinking to make a capture, on coming in sight near a family dwelling. The family seeing them, set up a loud noise through fear there would be a fight, which placed all parties on the guard. They (the cavalry) saw many persons, appearantly engaged about fires in the act of cooking and other occupations.

The Scouts, thinking they had droped in a hornets nest, the better part of valor to withdraw quietly which they did. Not a gun fired by either party.

Smith while about, would send in word he was the provost Marshal of that road. No one to pass that way without his order, and many such impertinent threats in this way. He was permitted to remain long as he wished. Some times he was seen near the Salem pike bridge riding about leisurely.

During his rounds he called at the house of Mr. P., calling at the gate, which was refused. Finally going out. Says he. Have you taken the oath? Answering in the affirmative. Where is it? In my pocket. Let me see it. Shewing the oath to him. Now eat that oath up, and that d-d quick. P. commenced tearing off small bits of paper and chewing. Thus he continued untill the whole was finished. It was dry chewing and swallowing, but no getting off as a pistol was ready cocked, and in case of refusal it would be used. He was under the impression after eating the oath Smith would kill him, as there had been a dislike a year or two past. The family interfered and prevailed on him not to interfere further, which he consented to, then riding off.

1864—De Witt Smith Captured

The man Smith after some time was captured. He had been ranging the neighborhood since he killed the old man at his house. Two young men wishing to take him for the Yankees. It was the intention to get the advantage by pretending to be friends of his, having formed some intimacy with each other.

This takes place at Nolensville. It was proposed they take a ride as friends. After going some distance on the road a demand of him to surrender to them. This he refused. Drawing a pistol, shot one of the friends. The other firing at Smith, wounding in the face. He fell from his horse. The one firing last fled, returning to town, secreting himself in a house. Thus the statement.

Smith, after lying in the road some time from the stun of the shot, recovering sufficently. He also returns to the same place, commencing a search for the man that shot him. Finding the wherabouts, walks in, and commences firing at and wounding him. Then taking fire for the purpose of burning the house, which was with difficulty prevented. He threatning to shoot any one that would stop him. The woman of the house beging him not to fire it. He was fully determined and continued his efforts.

Some person from the opposite street with a double barrel shot gun, fired a load buck shot at him, mortally wounding him. The next day he was sent for and brought to Murfreesboro in a dying condition. He lived about three days after and died, his wounds being greatly agravated hauling over a rough road.

It was not certain what would be done with him. There were various reports about the streets. One, on the Monday following he would be taken out and hung. Whether true or not the Yankees were so much exasperated at him they were ready to commit almost any act, even to hang a half killed man.

It was clearly seen the negros were greatly disappointed by loosing the chance of seeing a man hung.

The relations of the young man were not permitted to see him when alive. He was kept in the court house untill his death. His remains were given to the friends, taken home and buried.

Thus, ends the life of one of the most reckless, daring young men of the age.

The Sequel

One of the most atrocious murders ever committed by any claiming to be civilized in any country, as related.

The murder committed on the person, a young man name Jobe of this county, whose parents live in the neighborhood of Eagleville. He and two other friends of the Confederate army making convenient to visit their homes and friends. They were out as Scouts.

By some means information is given they are in the neighborhood. A small scouting party is sent out to capture them. Going to the place they are supposed to be, they find Jobe, the other two being absent. They take him in the woods, there commence a course of torture in every conceivable manner to make him inform where the other two are. They could get nothing that would give a clue. He was whiped with switches, hang him a short time, then let him down. Still getting no information.

He told them he was in their power. They may punish as they see proper. May kill him. It was all they could do. He was determined to reveal nothing to them, trying every way. They broke his arms and legs, split his tongue. To make a finish he was hung to a limb of a tree, leaving word where the friends may find him if they wish.

A Lieutenant pointed out as one of the inquisitors. This officer telling most of the circumstances, the balance telling for itself. He also stated the young man was one of the bravest, determined men he ever met with.

To carry out the supposition leading to the death of the old man Burgess. He lived in the neighborhood of Smith's father. It was known he had been giving information and it was supposed he had in this case given the where-abouts and doings of the young men, causing the arrest.

Smith and friend avenge the death of Jobe on the person Burgess. He was heard to use the expression that they will retaliate to the fullest extent in their power.

Hood Raid

During the time Genl. Hood was on the way to Nashville, Genl. Forrest with his command of cavalry, was on the road to Murfreesboro, arriving in the neighborhood about the 7th of Decem. to make a demonstration on this post. Before his arrival the Federals has largely reinforced by the addition of Genls. Russeau and Millroy. The gov. stores and goods belonging to the citizens had been moved from town to the forts, to have them protected in case of an attact on the town.

Forrests main force make their appearance on the Salem pike about three miles from town, sending a portion round to different points to feel the enemy. While occupying this position the Federal cavalry was sent to make an attact on him on the extreme left of the Stones River ground. The two forces meet and a spirited battle ensues, lasting some length of time, both holding about the same ground for several hours with losses to each. Toward night firing ceased gradually untill the two commands retired from the field.

A detachment of confederates make their appearance on the east and south east of town, coming within the limits, planting some pieces of artillery and commenced a vigerous shelling of the place. It was said to be a Missippi regiment. They threw some forty or fifty shots in town in different directions, doing but little damage more than striking a fiew houses. Two shots striking the court house. One or two striking Lawings Cabinet Shop. One near the Methodist church. Several others in this vicinity. None of the shells bursting. No one killed by these shots. The firing lasted in this direction some time. This was a wanton piece of destruction. Nothing to be gained by the confederates in thus shelling the town. The federal troops were all at the forts. Nothing remaining in town but citizens and many of them at the forts guarding property.

In the mean time Gen. Rosseau came from the fort with a detachment of artillery. During the shelling of the confederates, advancing up College Street. Planting his cannon commenced returning the fire. In a short time the confederate battery was silenced, having one of the gun carriages disabled.

In the cannon duel one man belonging to the confederate battery had both legs broken. One or two others wounded. One federal soldier killed near the cemetary by a cannon ball. This was about the causalities this time.

The confederates came down East Main Street far as Januarys Infirmary, remaining there but a short time, then falling back to another position.

Skirmishing continued round Murfreesboro for several days after which it ceased. The confederates retreating in the direction of Franklin, covering the retreat of Gen. Hood from Nashville.

The causalities during the raid, from the best information gathered—of the federal will aproximate to one hundred and fifty killed and wounded. About one third on the killed list. No cannon lost. On the confederate side could not have been much as no reports to that effect. In all not exceeding twenty.

The federal force at this place were generally new troops. Many never had been in battle. Such soldiers generally shoot high, doing little effect, probably a fortunate thing for the confederates on this occaision.

The confederates did considerable damage to the R. Road between this place and Nashville, tearing up the rails and timber and throwing in piles and burning, rendering the iron useless for road purpose. Nearly all the block houses on the road were vacated. The Depot at Lavergne was cleaned out. The great number of negro houses that was in and round the place were burned. Nothing remaining but the chimneys to tell of the late flourishing vilage. The negros scattered to the four winds.

It may be attributed to the gallantry of Gen. Rosseau for the safety of the town from a distructive shelling from the forts. He happening there just in time to prevent the unnecessary work. Gen. Vancleave, the post commander, had just issued orders for shelling. The men were preparing for the task and pleased with the idea. They had been often promised should the rebels make their appearance in town it should be shelled to pieces.

When Gen. Rosseau came up making enquiry, what are you going to do Genl.? I'm going to shell the rebels out of the town. There is no use in that. It is our town. We must not destroy it! Give me a detachment of men and cannon. I will drive them off. The request was granted after some hesitation on the part of Gen. Vancleave. He came and in a short time the matter was all set right. No property destroyed as would have been firing at the rebels. By timely interference of Rosseau the town saved from shelling and probably the life of many citizens.

During the raid an order was out to strip the plank from garden and yard fences of the citizens to make field hospitals, a thing not needed at the time as they were amply supplyed. However, fences, stables, and yards were striped and hauled off, giving the town quite a naked appearance, a mode of annoyance.

Wheel-barrows, spades, and picks did not miss. Wagons were sent to all dwellings collecting these articles. This was supplying the commissary lossage of such articles, as he is chargable with things missing.

Gen. Millroy

Gen. Millroy was among the commanders at this place. He had the name of being a tyranical man in his way, having little respect as to rights of people. His habit was having citizens arrested for some supposed injury, imprisoned, sometimes having them condemned to be shot or hung, under the plea they were "bushwhackers." Generally unpopular in all sections where may have been placed. While he was at this place he took possession of a citizens dwelling for his head quarters, ordering the family out. They to leave every thing in the house as it was. No argument could stop him. They must go and leave things in his charge and use. In such cases soldiers usually helped themselves to what suited them. Fortunately, his stay in Murfreesboro was short.

Incidence at Murfreesboro

During the time the raid was going on round the town there were many singular acts done by the people in it. Caused through fear of some supposed danger.

From the movements of the negros one would suppose the day of judgement had commenced. They were flying in all directions with bundles on their heads and under arms. Some without any thing, muttering half prayer and half cry, casting up accounts of past doings. All anxious to claim some one, master or mistress. They had been at home all the time, insisting "if da com, say I b'longs to you, has been here all de time." A great change came over the negros that was wearing the loyal blue, presto and all were in old "butter nut" coats and pants, walking about pretending to be engaged at ordinary business.

The negros generally having great fears of being caught by Forrest. His name was a terror to them.

Capt. Campbell in a Fight

The Capt. was commander of a squad of Yankee cavalrys. A brave man in a saloon fight. Not afraid to attact two or three men at a time. In a knock down and drag out "Sesesh" would be no where in his hands. Almost demolish a whole company at short notice. His boys would hollow for him "Bully for you!"

However, on the day of the attact at this place he is seen passing down the street with three or four others, looking pale as if he had just rissen from bed of a months sickness. He takes command of his men, gallops round a while, each man with the thumb on the cock of his gun to be in readiness. Going down the Lebanon pike a short distance dismount, one to hold five horses. They form a line. In a short time commence a vigerous fire toward the enemy over a half mile off. Supposing the battle beginning to grow hot and heavy they change position. From two to four croud behind trees and stumps, still firing in the direction of the enemy.

To an observer it would appear the Capt. was fighting the men on his own account. The enemy too far off to drive a bullet to them. The rebels were posted near the University on the east. Capt. Campbells command on the Lebanon pike north of town, more than a half mile, and a number of houses between the two. The rebels not aware the Capt. was fighting them so valiently. However, after battling away in this manner some time, he drew off his men without loss.

Genl. Vancleave

The post commander, like a hen on a hot griddle, was moving about during the time, in an anxious manner. Scarcely knowing what to do, like Bill Acres whose valor was oozing out at the ends of his fingers. However, having with him a friend, Mr. C., who kept up his courage at the trying moment. It appears during the investment of the town by the rebels, a flag of truce was sent. When on the way from the rebels, for exchange of prisoners. The announcement was made. The Genl. thinking it a demand of a surrender, taking a long breath with a kind of gasp, says he to the friend "What had I best do?" Had I better surrender the post or fight? By this time the flag arrives. The business made known, which was for exchanging men. The genl. now breathing more easy. Agrees to the proposition. Immediately gladly making the exchange.

Confederate Prisoners 1865

About the 20th Decem. there were about one hundred and fifty confederate prisoners in Murfreesboro. Many of them in a verry destitute condition for the want of clothing and shoes. The ladys were permitted to furnish what clothing they were able to procure. Such articles most wanted were difficult to get. However, they collected old clothes and repaired them for the soldiers. Sometimes the Yankees were disposed to be contrary letting the articles thus prepared be taken in.

The whole of the prisoners were kept in one room in the Cumberland Church. At times when provisions was sent to the soldiers by the women, the guards would frequently take a greater share before it was delivered. After being kept some time at this place, they were sent north to prison.

About the close of the year there were quite a number leaving the army, coming home, and giving themselves up and taking the required oath, regarding the whole matter as a lost cause. The past fiew days has been extremely cold causing great suffering with the soldiers.

January 1865

The morning of the first opened extremely cold. The thermometer on the day previous was ranging at 40°. During the night it had fallen to 8°.

After the Hood raid had subsided the people began to be more hopeful of better times. Many looking on the late demonstration as a failure. This was not only the feeling of the people of Rutherford, it was general over the state. Under this view of the matter many of the counties hold conventions, appointing delegates to meet a general convention at Nashville, to devise ways to reestablish a form of civil government. At first it was a feeble effort, yet it continued to gain strength, notwithstanding the doubts of many people of the propriety of the move, in consequence of the great number of the soldiery in the country.

The day for meeting of the convention at Nashville arrives. Rutherford sending a large delegation as representatives. Of the great number of delegates in attendance at the convention, many of them were self constituted out of the refugees that were whilling away their times at Nashville to keep out of service. The convening of the members of the convention takes place about the 10th Jany.

After the convention was organized the speaker appointed. The next thing in order was secretary. Mr. Sherbrook of Rutherford was proposed and elected, feeling greatly flattered by the honors conferred. After time Mr. F. performs a conspiceous part in setting the old ship of state afloat and establishing law and order in the land.

The convention feeling encouraged. They resolved to organize themselves into a state convention and make nominations. For Gov. W.G. Brownlow, Senator for Williamson and Rutherford; William Spence, Representative W.Y. Elliott, Rutherford; James Mullins, Floater for Rutherford and Bedford; William Bosson, citizen of Rutherford and Senator of White.

All the counties having men appointed by the convention as candidates, to make a safe thing that all should be voted for. It was on the general ticket. On this system a voter voted for the whole of the legislature at the same time.

Men were appointed to hold elections as sheriffs of the different counties. Mr. Sherbrook was for Rutherford. The first election set for the 4th March for Gov. and members.

The Times

The winter weather continues unusually cold. About the last of January and first of February 1865 ice formed five inches thick, affording opportunity of filling houses.

It was comparitively quiet times about Murfreesboro, considering the great number of soldiers in and around the place. The people were having a rough time procuring provisions and wood. Every thing in that way was at the highest notch. Marketing brought to town was guarded to the commissary store. They purchase what they want at their own price. If any over the citizens have a small chance for supplying themselves. Not before.

The Yankee soldiers are comfortably housed in their shantys erected round the court house yard. They are having an easy time when not on duty. Many of them are occupied making trinkets of mussel shells from the river near the battlefield. These articles were made as memorials of the great battle of Stones river. The officers also had the appearance and manner of men that would prefer the war to continue on, provided they were kept out of danger.

Quite a number of Yankee farmers who are disposed to engage in the business of raising cotton. They are importing implements and making bargains with the negros for the season. They think a fortune is to be made at the business of raising cotton.

The negros were not much disposed to make contracts to work for others. It was their wish to set up for themselves, they having the belief the lands of the country was to be divided in small parcels of forty acres and given to those having families.

Negros in blue cloths. They were in the habit of wearing cast off soldier's clothing. The Yankees ordering those in this dress to be reported to the pro. marshal, unless in the government employ. All brass buttons cut off. Also ordered to find employment in the country. They were a little hard on Sambo.

Election in Tennessee 1865

According to the time set by the convention an election was held over the state for members to the legislature. Also, ratifying the constitution as amended in January. There were about twenty three thousand votes polled at this election, all voting one way, there being no opposition in the race. Each voter voting for all the members of legislature.

The people of Rutherford were quite indifferent. The votes polled in the county was light. The general impression among the people, the move was rather premature. War still going on and what would be done would amount to little.

Mr. Sherbrook acting sheriff in the election, according to the appointment of the convention. Also, wishing to shew the people his loyalty to the government. The county sheriff's power at this time was ignored. Merely a looker on.

Negro Anniversary

The great day (March 4th) came with the negros. The town is crouded with them from the country to celebrate the anniversary of their freedom. They are dressed out in their best. Some appearantly dressed within an inch of life. Sashes and various badges to set them off. Marshals on horse back dashing about. Others on foot.

The body form a line of six deep. The first section filled with able bodied men, carrying implements of their various occupations, hoes, axes, saws, shoe-makers lasts, and other articles. The next section, school children finely dressed, and ornamented with badges. There were about three hundred of these. Then came the women, all in a body, in their finest appearance. To complete stragglers to fill the line. Old men, women and children, and anything else that were disposed to follow.

At the head of the column there are drums and fifes to give the affair a martial appearance, together with a large flag "old Stars and Stripes," interspersed with numerous smaller flags along the line. The whole line headed by two colored chaplains, with others on horse back. Thus formed, the order is given to move. The band of music strike up some lively air, having a variety of variations of sounds and tones, bending their course to Murfrees Spring, where preparation is made for speeches. The marshals were prompt in keeping the column in order. "Ladys an gem'men, keep strait dar in de line." After which the whole procession is followed by chaplain Earnshaw, P.V. Marshall Hill, Commissioner Sherbrook, Pro. Bush, and the Yankee teacher school marms, and a host of soldiers keeping up the rear.

After the procession arrive at the ground Chaplain Earnshaw takes the stand, letting off a speech in an eloquent manner, contrasting the situation of the colored people with what it had been. Changing from slavery to freedom. They are this day celebrating the anniversary or first year of freedom. They must act like free men and women, have an education and rise in the scale of inteligence. After continuing his advisory speech some length to the colored citizens, he concluded his remarks.

Mr. Hill next on the stand. He congratulates the colored friends on the present happy occaision. Leading off in a short speech, giving advice how they should conduct themselves in future. Reminding them it was a glorious day which they were celebrating and long to be remembered by their race.

Mr. Sherbrook, not wishing to be thought neglectful at the time, he mounts the stand and calling attention, "I wish to say fiew words to the colored friends. I have been their strongest friend in the convention at Nashville, advocating their freedom. I feel happy to day to see they are enjoying the privilege of free men and women and they also have an opportunity offered for an education, so they may become good citizens of the country. But, before I conclude, I would say to the colored friends, I am keeping a grocery store on the public square where I shall be pleased to see you all. I will sell lower than any of the rebel houses. Dont expect to make much. It is more for your accommodation." After delivering himself of this speech, he then took a chew of tobacco. Looking round over the croud, stepped down with the satisfaction he had accomplished much.

Beside there was speeches by colored orators. The day was spent pleasantly. Toward evening they again formed a procession, marched back to town and were dismissed.

Lee Surrender

News reached Murfreesboro of the surrender of Genl. Lee and his army on April 9th to Gen. Grant. This news caused great rejoicing with the union men. Every thing was life and animation with them. Minute guns were fired at the forts the whole day. The church bells rang during the day. Steam whistles blowing and any thing else calculated to make a noise in the way of rejoicing. At night a great demonstration of fire works. There were an overflowing of the Yankee feeling generally. Beside this bonfires, torch light procession after night. Also speaking by many of the officers. Many witty remarks at the expense of "Sesesh."

At that meeting there was one peculiar personage, one of the most patriotic Southern men, who packed up and fell back with Bragg for the purpose of cutting and making, not shooting and killing. His time all devoted "for the good of the soldiers." Somewhat familiar with the history with the four kings, a favorite amusement with him while in the army. At times he would swing round in a happy manner, affirm he was devoted to the poor soldiers. No one doubted his loyalty to the south. However, he disappeared mysteriously from the army, traveling a thousand miles out of the way to reach home. After he came he was taken through the necessary purification.

At the demonstration of the surrender, where speeches were made, our hero felt somewhat inspired. Wishing to shew he was deeply imbued with the feeling of patriotism, mounts a dry goods box in the street, with hat in hand waving round his head, crying out at the top of his voice, "Three cheers for the down fall of Richmond!"

At these times it was necessary to have a permit from the board of trade to do business. This was an opportunity of making our hero popular with the Yankees, thus introducing himself a truly loyal man. He afterward did a thriving business in his line.

Federal Soldiers Mustered Out July 1865

About the first July, a large body of union soldiers stationed about Murfreesboro, are on the move for home to be discharged from service. A number of soldiers wishing to take with them some memento of services in the war. Their wits were greatly put to the test to make a proper selection. The christian commissions and chaplains having been a head, they had appropriated all that was rare that they could lay hands on and spirited it away months ago.

However, they determine to get up a menagery on a small scale. The most suitable curiosity to astonish the gaping crouds of natives who will come by thousands to see the veterans returning from the war.

A specimen seen at the R R Depot leaving, soldiers loaded down with their guns, napsacks and blankets. Numbers of them with dogs, some one, others with two. They are of all sizes, and appearance. Some with cages containing Raccoons, Squirrels, birds of various kinds, supposed to be the mawking bird they had been nursing some weeks past. Cedar fancy boxes and cedar walking sticks made of the wood from the Stones River battle ground and many other curious things which they had collected during the stay. These mememtos will be kept in families of old soldiers to amuse the little urchins round their knees, telling of their exploits fighting for the restoration of the Old Stars and Stripes to the union. The little fellows sitting with mouth and eyes open, listening to the thrilling narrative of the heroic pop, wondering what kind of people the "Sesesh" are, whether they walk on two or four feet.

Confederate Soldiers Coming Home 1865

About the 15th July, 1865, the confederate soldiers are daly arriving in small squads. They had been scattered over all parts of the country. Some coming from prisons of the north, all generally a thread-bare appearance both in looks and clothing. Of the latter, all they had was what they were wearing, yet they enjoyed good health.

All were glad the war had closed, still regretted they were compelled to surrender the cause. The feeling of some were inclined to leave the country. Now at their ruined homes, having nothing to do and worst of all nothing to do with. The season had so far advanced for field labor the prospect for making a crop was anything but promising to those who engage in that employment, and scarcely any demand for mechanical labor.

A marked difference between the two classes of soldiers (Yankee and Rebel) on their return home. One loaded down to the guards (to use a batman phrase) with plunder, relicts and dogs, homeward bound. Wheels submerged, with difficulty they move. While the other freighted light and running high with difficulty. The wheels touch water enough to move. One, an adventurer in search of fortune by the miseries of war. The other, an adventurer for supposed rights to be gained by the same process.

Also, a number of citizens arriving by two and three at a time who had been off refugeeing in the south. They are dumping their trunks, looking round for some familiar place, once a home. But how disappointed, scarcely a vestage or stick to mark the spot, while other cramed with Negros to overflowing, windows stoped with cast off soldier cloths.

Raising the Old Flag—Sept. 1865

An officer going round among those in business soliciting money to purchase a flag. No one disposed to shew unwillingness to subscribe. The amount necessary was raised, also a flag pole. The flag was twenty by thirty six feet. The pole, which was for the occaision (broke in the attempt to raise) was one hundred and twenty feet long. In consequence of the failure of the flag staff the dome of the court house was used for the present occaision.

Notice being given for Saturday, May 13th for raising the flag, and that all business houses suspend at two oclock, for the purpose of celebrating the raising the old Stars and Stripes.

Appearance of things after the close of war—1865.

The federal army had all returned home except a fiew gov. officers remaining to wind up business, selling stock and closing out commissary departments.

Among the removals was Gen. Vancleave, which the people were gratified to know. He held the place as post commander more than a year. Had he been brave he would have been more generous. He was not popular with the people as many other officers that had been about during war.

The Southern Soldiers had returned to their homes, feeling anxious to get employment for a living.

The government officers are busied collecting and selling all articles in their use, from saw mills, down to a horse nail at auction. Things thus sold was knocked off at a great sacrifice to the bidder. Those having money to invest in this way was likely to make it profitable.

We now take a view of town as it appeared. Murfreesboro was held as a military point during the war. By the close things was in a confused condition. The best houses were used and much abused by the military power during the stay. Numbers of houses were either burned or pulled down, they said to make field hospitals, but never made. This was done to destroy and annoy the people.

The brick wall round the court yard pulled down. The jail house burned which had been a quartering of negros, it having been vacant some time as a prison. The market house on the north side of the public square had disappeared. The business rooms on the public square were used for commissary stores. There was a hospital established in the three store rooms on the north east corner of the public square, the counters and shelving taken out. Fences round dwelling lots near all destroyed. A fiew exceptions. Scarcely a whole fence to be seen in town. Wagons passing all directions over lots and gardens.

Reburial of Confederate Dead

Among other things an effort was on foot to collect and rebury the Confederate Soldiers lying scattered over the country, killed in battle and otherwise. It was a laudable undertaking and proper to be done, yet the people were little able to stand the expense necessary. However, the Ladies, not willing the object should fail in paying proper respect to the confederate dead. They form a Society, calling it a Memorial Society of Murfreesboro. Having elected officers for the proper management of the Society, they then commenced collecting contributions. In the course of time a sufficient amount was raised to purchase a piece of land to establish a confederate cemetery. The grounds were neatly enclosed and handsomly laid off in squares and graded walks, ornamented with evergreen shrubbery. The graves in regular order in each square, with well painted head and foot boards, names of such as are known, others unknown.

Through the energy of Capt. Arnold who was employed, he collected and reintered several hundred remains from the battle fields and other points in these grounds.

Much credit is due to the Ladies of Murfreesboro for their untiring energy and perseverance in raising means to purchase grounds for the resting place of the bones of the lamented southern soldier, at a time when poverty swayed the land.

The Confederate Cemetery is about one mile South of town, lying between the R.R. and Shelbyville pike.

Looking round for those beautiful oak groves surrounding the town a short time since. All disappeared with the exception of a lonely tree here and there pointing to the once noble forest. Those permitted to remain because they "gessed it wont pay to cut them down." This timber the pride of the owners. This clearing of timber was carried out in the country more or less for three miles round. Plantations were stripped of fences. Scarcely a wagon load of good rails to be found. Cedar rails hauled to town by the thousand for fuel. All the effects of war.

The prospect was gloomy to those returning from the war without any thing to make a commencement, with little credit and less money.

INDEX

A

Anderson, Col. 5
Anniversary of Negro Freedom 157, 158
Apology 1
Arnold, Captain 161

B

Baldwin, S.D. 39, 40
Banks, Gen. 142
Battle of Stones River 58-65
Beauregard, Gen. Gustave 24, 27, 66
Bell, John 2
Bell, John Jr. 86
Bohmes, J. 6
Bosson, William 156
Bowie Knife 31
Brack, James 92, 110, 111, 112, 113
Bragg, General 50-63, 82, 85, 90, 93, 107, 108, 109, 115
Breckinridge, General John 2
Brownlow, Gov. 156
Buchanan, Gov. John P. 3, 4
Buckner, Gen. Bolivar 16
Buell, Gen, Don Carlos 8, 9, 16, 23, 24, 40, 51-54, 65, 66, 122
Burgess, Mr. 151
Burk, Adjutant 84
Burton's Law Books 104
Butler, Gen. Benjamin 26

C

Campbell, Gen. William 125, 154
Carney, L.H. 86
Carney, Mrs. L.H. 13
Chase, S.P. 125
Chattanooga (Battle of) 108, 109
Chickamauga (Battle of) 98, 99
Childress, John W. 20
Confederate Cemetery 161
Confederate States of America 3
Cooper, E. 32
Corinth (Battle of) 26, 27, 28
Cothran, James 38
Cowan, Esquire 57
Covington, Mr. 129
Crittenden, Gen. George 14, 45, 48
Crockett, Mr. 140
Currins, R. 86

D

Davis, Pres. Jeff 124
Douglas, Stephen 2
Duffer, W.C. 31
Duffield, Gen. 44, 46

E

Earnshaw, Chaplain 158
Elliott, W.G. 156

F

Fishing Creek (Battle of) 14
Forrest, Gen. Nathan Bedford ... 13, 36, 43, 44, 45, 46, 47, 48, 49, 50, 52, 56, 133, 140, 141, 148
Fort Donelson 9, 10, 15, 16, 17
Fort Henry 10, 15
Fort Pillow 8, 141
Fortress, Rosecrans 73, 74, 80, 83, 84, 85, 86, 108

G

Garrett, W.G. 7
Grant, Gen. U. 134, 137, 138, 150, 158
Grapevine Telegraph 41
Gun Boats 14

H

Hagan, Mrs. 48
Haines, Ivy 29, 30
Harris, Gov. Isham 4
Henderson, Mr. 139
Hewitt, Capt. 36, 46
Hill, Provost Marshall 158
Home Guards of Murfreesboro 29
Hood, Gen. John Bell 152, 153, 155

J

James, F. 60
Jobe, Dee 151, 152
Johnson, Gov. Andrew 23, 32
Johnson, Gen. J.E. 115, 124
Johnston, Gen. A.S. ... 16, 17, 18, 20, 23, 24, 25, 66

K

Keeble, Mr. 139
King, Dr. 13

L

Lazarus 131, 132
Lee, Gen. R.L. .. 10, 66, 94, 95, 137, 138, 158
Lester, Col. 36, 39, 46
Lick, John 29
Lincoln, Pres. Abraham 2, 3, 4, 6, 77, 107, 124, 125, 134
Longstreet, Gen. 98
Lytle, W.F. 86

M

Manassas (Battle of) 10-12

163

McClelland, Gen. 10, 66, 122, 125
McCook, Gen. 65
Maney, D. 86
Market Quotations 123
Mead, Gen. 94, 95
Memphis (Battle of) 26
Menefee, Mr. 38
Mercer (Editor) 39
Miller, A. 12
Millroy, Gen. 152, 154
Mitchell, Addison 7
Mitchell, Gen. 19, 20, 21, 34, 35
Missionary Ridge (Battle of) 109
Morgan, Gen. John H. 18, 23, 56, 98, 117, 118
Mullins, James .156
Mustering Out of Federal Troops 159

N

Nelson, Josiah (Daughter Shot) 100
Negro Military Company 108, 129
Negro School 110, 111, 112
Nesbitt, Mr. (Citizen Shot During
Forrest Raid) 48
New Orleans (Taken by Federals) 26
Northcutt (Editor) 39

P

Palmer, Gen. J.B. 7, 16, 60, 104, 140
Parkhurst, Gen. 20, 22, 33, 34, 36, 37
Patterson, H.A. 91, 92, 103-105, 110-112, 130, 139
Perryville, Ky. (Battle of) 53, 54
Pierce Mill 43
Pittsburg Landing (Battle of) 23, 24, 25
Polk, Gen. 99
Providence Church 92
Pugh, H.S. 49

R

Ransom, William 29, 140
Ready, Charles 86
Robertson, T. 6
Rosecrans, General 54, 56-66, 79, 90, 93, 95, 96, 98, 99, 105, 107, 116
Rounds, O.C. . .20, 22, 33, 37, 38, 39, 48, 108
Rousseau, Gen. 152, 153

S

Sanders, Richard 6
Saw Mills 116
Secession of Southern States 3
Sherbrook, Mr. 156, 157, 158
Shiloh (Battle of) 23, 24, 25
Sickles, Simon 31
Sly, David 82, 83
Smallpox 115
Smith, DeWitt 148-151
Smith, Gen. 29, 30, 56
Spence, William .156

T

Tennessee Votes to Secede 9
Thomas, Gen. 99, 107

U

Union University (As A Hospital) 13
United Christian Commission 96

V

Van Cleve, Gen. 94, 146
Van Dorn, Gen. 79
Verner, Lucy 135, 136
Vicksburg (Battle of) 93, 95

W

Wheeler, Gen. 57, 66, 99, 100, 101, 102, 110, 145, 146, 147
White, Stephen 6
Wilder, Gen. 99, 100, 101, 102
Winston, Sam 29

Y

Yankee Slang Words 76, 77

Z

Zollicoffer, Gen. F.K. 14